# Visit
# The Musée d'Orsay

# SUMMARY

---

**Claude Monet**
*The Rue Montorgueil in Paris. Celebration of June 30*
(La Rue Montorgueil. Fête du 30 juin 1878)
1878, oil on canvas

*Cover:*
**Claude Monet**
*Woman with Parasol*
(Femme à l'ombrelle)
1886
oil on canvas

# VISIT THE MUSÉE D'ORSAY

Preface by Serge Lemoine, Managing Director of the Musée d'Orsay

The Musée d'Orsay is one of the most celebrated museums in the world. Devoted to the second half of the nineteenth century, since it opened in 1986, the museum owes its success to its exceptional collections in all artistic disciplines – painting, sculpture, furniture, *objets d'art*, architecture, drawing, photography – produced essentially between 1850 and 1914. Its originality is further enhanced by its installation in an unexpected venue, an old train station built in 1900 on the banks of the Seine, facing the Tuileries Gardens and the Louvre Museum. This choice setting, monumental and luminous, makes for a striking experience.

Sculpture is found right at the entrance, and statues positioned along the nave, laid out in tiers of steps, lead towards Carpeaux' original group of *The Dance* (La Danse) from the façade of Garnier's Opera House. Rodin and the later styles of Bourdelle, Joseph Bernard and Maillol can be admired on the terraces. The representation of movement or repose, whether in marble or bronze, individual statuettes or groups of figures, all forms of expression can be found here.

Then there are the paintings, works by the greatest artists of the period which can be explored throughout the museum, along both sides of the central walkway of the nave, in the cupola rooms on the middle level, or in the upper gallery, with its natural overhead lighting, opening out onto the Parisian landscape. The most illustrious names, Manet, Degas, Monet, Renoir, Cézanne, Seurat, Gauguin, Van Gogh, next to Millet, Courbet and Puvis de Chavannes, can be seen nearby those no less famous in their time, Gérôme, Jean-Paul Laurens, Tissot or Bastien-Lepage, in an effort to show all artistic trends to advantage. Impressionism as well Realism, Naturalism, Symbolism or the Nabis are thus placed in the artistic context of the time.

Among the museum's many masterpieces one could mention Courbet's monumental *Burial at Ornans* (Un Enterrement à Ornans) with its frieze-like composition and brutality of expression; the sculptural figures of Millet's *The Angelus* (L'Angélus), a nineteenth-century icon; Puvis de Chavannes' *The Poor Fisherman* (Le Pauvre Pêcheur) with forms simplified to the extreme, one of the most innovative paintings of the century which was to inspire so many artists, from Gauguin to Picasso; the shockingly violent contrasts of Manet's *Olympia*, the nude which created a scandal; Monet's *Magpie* (La Pie), arresting for the novelty of the expression of light and shadow; the surprising construction of Cézanne's *Woman with Coffee Pot* (Femme à la cafetière); Seurat's *Circus* (Le Cirque) which displays all the possibilities of the new technique of 'pointillism'; and the charmingly

**Vincent Van Gogh**
*Midday* or *The Siesta*
(La Méridienne
*ou* La Sieste)
1889-1890
oil on canvas

original composition of Degas' pastel *The Tub* (Le Tub).

Covering all disciplines, the Musée d'Orsay also offers sets of furniture and exceptional individual pieces in the field of the decorative arts, where Art Nouveau is illustrated through works by Gallé and Guimard. The field of architecture is shown to great advantage in its own exhibition space where scale models accompany drawings and original plans by the great builders of the age, from Garnier to Eiffel.

The Musée d'Orsay also holds a substantial collection of photography ranging from its invention in 1839 through to the 1920s. Since October 2002, this art form, born in the nineteenth century, has been on perma-

nent exhibition through regularly updated presentations. From Charles Nègre to Alfred Stieglitz by way of Atget, Nadar and many others, the history of this medium is illustrated through more than 50,000 images.

Finally, a drawings gallery will allow the museum to better display its collection through thematic exhibitions.

Our view of nineteenth-century art never ceases to evolve. Today, contemporary artists are invited to display their work, in connection with a piece of art of their choice from the Orsay collections, reminding us that the artists of the nineteenth century are still a lively source of inspiration for contemporary art.

Serge Lemoine

# 1

# A Museum
# in a Train Station

# A Museum in a Train Station

"The train station is superb and looks like a Palais des Beaux-Arts," wrote the painter Édouard Détaille in 1900. From this palatial station, after having housed the Renaud-Barrault Theatre, a hotel and the Company of Auctioneers, the Musée d'Orsay was to be born.

The Musée d'Orsay, this place of intense sensations, where loses oneself amid emotions and passions, poetry and melancholy, daydreaming and discovery, has since 9 December 1986 welcomed nearly fifty million visitors. In the heart of Paris, it enjoys an exceptional location on the left bank of the Seine, facing the Tuileries Gardens, not far from the Louvre and the *Place de la Concorde*.

Once the estate of Queen Marguerite, in the eighteenth century this became one of the most sought-after neighbourhoods of the aristocracy, the location of sumptuous private townhouses such as the *Hôtel de Salm* (today the Musée de la Légion d'Honneur) built between 1782 and 1788. In 1810, Napoleon I decided to build the *Palais d'Orsay*, allocated to the *Cour des Comptes* (Court of Accounts) and the *Conseil d'État* (State Council). It was adorned with one of Théodore Chassériau's most beautiful decorative cycles, *Peace, War and Commerce* (La paix, la guerre et le commerce, Louvre Museum), partially saved from the fire which ravaged the building during the height of the bloody events of the 1871 Commune. The ruins remained in place until 1898. Any idea of restoration was quickly abandoned and the construction of a future museum of decorative arts was considered. It was for this project that, Auguste Rodin received the commission, in 1890, for *The Gates of Hell* (La Porte de l'Enfer) whose original plaster cast can be seen today in the Musée d'Orsay.

## The birth of a train station

At the time of the 1900 World Fair, the Orleans railroad company felt its Austerlitz station was too remote and planned to build a new one. The idea caused deep disquiet: there were fears of a noisy, crude industrial building disfiguring one of Paris' most beautiful neighbourhoods. To put an end to the criticisms, the company consulted three architects of unassailable reputation: Émile Bénard, Lucien Magne and Victor Laloux (1850-1937), who in April 1898 won the competition. The winner of the 1878 Grand Prix de Rome, Laloux had already built the Saint Martin Basilica, the city hall and the train station in his hometown of Tours. The twofold challenge before him was to construct a building that could accommodate great numbers of travellers fit in the heart of historic Paris. For this reason, the industrial great hall of metal and glass, 32 metres high and 128 metres long, is masked by a very imposing stone façade. Construction went quickly and the station was opened on 14 July 1900. It was the first modern train station, designed for electric locomotion, which explains the luxurious look of the nave, decorated with sculpted and painted plaster casts reminiscent of a basilica or great Roman baths. The ballroom and restaurant of the 370-room hotel which completed the construction attest to the stateliness of the building. The architect designed every detail of the decor in a luxurious, eclectic style and commissioned official artists to carry out the designs: Fernand Cormon for the paintings in the departure hall; for the restaurant, Gabriel Ferrier whose *Allegory of the Periods of Time* (Allégorie des périodes du temps) features on the

ceiling, and Benjamin Constant (*The Routes of the Air*, Les routes de l'air); for the ballroom Pierre Fritel (*Apollo's Chariot*, Le Char d'Apollon). Three great sculptures symbolising the cities of Toulouse, by Laurent Marqueste, Bordeaux, by Jean-Baptiste Hugues, and Nantes, by Jean-Antoine Injalbert, were placed along the façade overlooking the Seine.

## From train station to museum

"The station is superb and looks like a *Palais des Beaux-Arts*, and since the *Palais des Beaux-Arts* looks like a train station, I suggest Laloux swaps them, if there's still time," wrote the painter Edouard Détaille! Eighty-six years later this inadvertent prophecy came true.

The station was rapidly outdated and service ended on 23 November 1939, while the hotel closed its doors for good in 1973. Demolition, which had been planned for 1971, was avoided at the cost of a crime against architecture: the destruction of Baltard's halls and all the emotion this caused... Listed in the *Inventaire supplémentaire des Monuments historiques* (Supplementary Inventory of Historic Monuments), it became the home to the Renaud-Barrault Theatre, in 1974, and the Company of

**Installation in the museum of Carpeaux'** *The Dance* **in 1986**
© J. Purcell / Musée d'Orsay

Auctioneers, while the *Direction des Musées de France* developed its proposal for the site: A museum was to be established in which all forms of art from the second half of the nineteenth century to the early twentieth century would be represented, creating a link with the Louvre and the collections of the *Musée National d'Art Moderne*. The plan was approved by Georges Pompidou and received the support of presidents Valéry Giscard d'Estaing and François Mitterrand. In 1979, a team of architects (Renaud Bardon, Pierre Colboc, Jean-Paul Philippon) of ACT Architecture won the State competition. The plans provided for the museum entrance on the *Rue de Bellechasse* and organised the collections all along the wide nave, opening it out to preserve its spaciousness. Above the galleries which line both sides of

the central walkway, terraces provide access on every floor to the cupolas of the old train station. On the top level, the roof area is laid out in one long gallery with natural lighting from above. The museum incorporates the reception rooms of the old hotel as well as the restaurant. Laloux's pillars, metal beams and stucco decor were respected throughout, restored and shown to advantage. There still remained the layout of the galleries, the design of their shapes, the choice of materials and colours, and the museographical furnishings. At the end of a period of consultation, in 1980, the Italian architect Gae Aulenti was awarded the job. She opted for a strong architectural style capable of holding its own in the vast space of the train station amid Laloux's decor. The museum galleries were unified through the use of

Buxy stone, a flambé limestone from Burgundy, on the floors and walls of all but the Impressionist Gallery. Colour-coding distinguishes the original metal structure, painted in green, from the added construction, in blue or brown.

### The symbol of an age

In addition to the specific time period it covers – three-quarters of a rich and fertile century – another of Orsay's unique aspects is its inclusion of a dedicated architecture (alongside painting and pastels, sculpture, decorative arts, photography and drawing). An expression of the aesthetics and techniques of the nineteenth century, building lends itself to an evocation of the types of work necessitated by the conditions of modern life, and of the very varied materials that were then in use as industry developed. Architecture has here been granted permanent exhibition spaces.

It would be impossible to cover all of the transformations undertaken by Napoleon III and the prefect of Paris, Eugène Haussmann. So Orsay has singled out the new Opera, built by Charles Garnier between 1861 and 1875. Emblematic of the Second Empire when it was begun, building was completed during the Third Republic. Carpeaux's sketches for *Dance* (La Danse), original models of the sculpted decor, stage set designs and two large modern models of this monument help to reconstitute its different aspects: urbanism, architecture and decor. The Amont Pavilion, an original space in its height, size and totally exposed metal structure, presents architectural grammar, the decorative vocabulary of the architect.

A gallery devoted to the exhibition of the drawing collections will soon be opened in order to do justice to those key figures of this flamboyant century, from Viollet-le-Duc to Gustave Eiffel, and from Victor Baltard to Hector Guimard.

Caroline Mathieu

**The baggage room, circa 1900**
© Fonds Urphot / Musée d'Orsay

**The transformation from train station to museum, 1984-1985**
© J. Purcell / Musée d'Orsay

# 2

# 1848:
# A Turning Point?

**Gustave Courbet**
*The Artist's Studio*
(L'Atelier du peintre)
1855
oil on canvas

**Auguste Clésinger**
*Woman Bitten by a Snake*
(Femme piquée
par un serpent)
1847, marble

# 2 | 1848: A Turning Point?

Orsay is the best place to gain an understanding of the situation
in the arts as Louis-Philippe gave way to the Republic.
Couture, Gérôme, Clésinger and above all Millet and Courbet
highlight the seamless shift from Romanticism to Realism
more than any rupture between them.

Around the year 1848, the situation of the arts in France was more than a little muddled. It has too often been said that the February Revolution dethroned Louis-Philippe and put an end to Romanticism all at the same time. As to Realism, it was supposed to be just simply another casualty of the Republican breakdown. The truth is that the art of Courbet and Millet, more receptive in any event to the rural world than to the urban working-class, is inseparable from the social climate of the 1840s and the evolution of Romanticism. What's more, it would be too simplistic to reduce the output and indeed the originality of the period from 1848 to 1870 down to these two names. The collections of the Musée d'Orsay in all creative fields, from painting to sculpture, from *objets d'art* to photography, allows one to understand that the road which apparently led from Delacroix to Manet was not a direct route exclusive of other developments whose repercussions were just as long-lasting. As we will see, there was also a classic modernity during these years. 1848 is not therefore a starting point in art history.

All contemporary writers described the artistic times which corresponded to the end of the July Monarchy and the start of the Second Republic as unsure, torn between tradition and opposing trends. The Salon, the great showcase of modern art in Paris, is the most visible and eloquent expression of

**Ernest Christophe**
*The Human Comedy* also known as *The Mask*
(La Comédie Humaine
*dit aussi* Le Masque)
1876, marble,
[ca. 1859)]

*Mr Couture's talent is naturally mundane […]
in the manner of Rembrandt […] and of
all the masters more curious about the true
than the beautiful, the real than the ideal.*

(Théophile Gautier, 1847)

**Thomas Couture**
*Decadent Romans*
(Romains
de la décadence)
1847, oil on canvas

this variety and even confusion. The last students of David, Romanticism in all its forms and the emergence of what the critics disdainfully called Realism – all were shown at the capital's most frequented exhibition of three thousand works, held every year since 1833. In 1853, it became a biennial but from 1863 was again an annual event. Official sanction or not, both the public and the critics were disconcerted by the impression the Salon gave that contemporary art had no real direction. In 1852, one shrewd critic was able to point to "this vagueness, how easily one goes from one direction to another, this eclecticism and cosmopolitanism, this voyage through every possible world, from the Byzantine to the daguerreotype, from deliberate mannerism to wilful brutality. One really feels there's something here to be done – but what? Is it a washerwoman or a dryad, a washbowl or a hero, a hovel or Olympus?"

## New Romanticism

In short, uncertainty spurred experimentation and the art of the time vacillated between plebeian garrets and antiquity revisited, Barbizon and the gilded Orient. Artists weren't afraid to mix the heroic and the familiar, historic events and scenes of daily life, with no regard for past conventions and prejudices. From its opening, the Musée d'Orsay has grouped together three of the most significant works in this overall mutation. It is hardly surprising that they were at the heart of an impassioned debate when they were shown at the 1847 Salon. As large as Veronese's *Wedding at Cana* (Noces de Cana) and colourful enough to be reminiscent of sixteenth-century Venetian painting, Thomas Couture's painting of *Decadent Romans* (Romains de la décadence) occupies a choice place in any visit to Orsay. Hanging near the large Courbets of 1850 to 1855, this finale of an ancient orgy expresses in its way

the artist's desire to renew historical painting through a greater attention to objectivity. An admirer of Gros and Géricault, those painters of national legend and exemplars of modern lyricism, Couture here sought to offer a new image of ancient Rome, no longer that of Republican virtue extolled by David around 1789, but of a society in decline, vice-ridden and as incapable of rejuvenation as the society of Louis-Philippe. That at least was Couture's diagnosis just months before the uprisings of February and June 1848. The heroes are tired. Historical painting which was supposed to be a noble expression and to capture irreproachable deeds had let itself be contaminated by romantic irony, by the rejection of ideal beauty and by social satire. Having conquered the world, the Roman Empire fell into a stupor... The response to this image of decline was to have been a large painting which Couture had sketched out in 1848 for the Republic. Of *The Volunteers of 1792* (Enrôlés volontaires de 1792) there remains only an enormous aborted canvas, imbued with the spirit of Michelet but hopelessly stuck, its momentum cut short. At the start of the Second Empire, Couture still though had a role to play in French painting. Dividing his time between religious subjects, works of fantasy and robust portraits, he welcomed into his studio a large number of young painters as promising as Manet.

**Jean-François Millet**
*The Angelus*
(L'Angélus)
1857
oil on canvas

**Rosa Bonheur**
*Ploughing in the Nivernais*
(Labourage nivernais,
le sombrage)
1849, oil on canvas

**Honoré Daumier**
*The Laundress*
(La Blanchisseuse)
1860-1861
oil on wood

## Modern Nudes

The same compromise between idealisation and realism can be seen in *Greek Youths Cock Fighting* (Jeunes Grecs faisant battre des coqs), another big hit of 1846. The setting is a Greece far removed from all moralising. For what is at stake in this fight to the death between two cocks is nothing less than the young woman, well-rounded and pale, seen in the foreground of this smooth painting, worrying, for good reason, about the outcome of the battle. This medium-scale work combines careful drawing and colouring with the liveliness of picturesque anecdote. "Under the fine pencil and delicate brush of Monsieur Gérôme, this apparently very common subject has taken on an exceptional elegance and exquisite distinction,"

wrote Gautier. Neo-Greek painters of the romantic idyll, so much in fashion in the years to follow, in its ultimate refinement, were not afraid of erotic undertones and the most audacious chromatic experimentation. Some time later, Gérôme was to evoke in his painting the pleasure houses of Pompeii… Finally, the 1847 Salon also introduced the public to another unknown. The young Clésinger, from the Franche-Comté like Courbet, exhibited his *Woman Bitten by a Snake* (Femme piquée par un serpent) with the open intention of attracting an aura of scandal to himself and his work. All throughout the nineteenth century, the Salon, through its huge size, was to attract this kind of publicity. With the passion of Romanticism and the memory of

**Jean-Léon Gérôme**
*Greek Youths Cock Fighting*
(Jeunes Grecs faisant battre des coqs)
1846, oil on canvas

Michaelangelo, Rubens as well as masters of French Rococo, Clésinger was able to set the marble in motion, with convulsions too suggestive not to cast doubt on the supposed pain of this modern nymph, in a state of undress, and with no mythological pretext; everyone at the time recognised the shapes if not the features of *Madame Sabatier*, the friend of Gautier and Baudelaire. Here too the great tradition of the nude, the very symbol of ideal perfection since the time of ancient Greece, clearly bowed to contemporary tastes. It should be remembered that these three works were considered too realist in their day and only the painting by Couture was immediately acquired by the State. It is true that in the eyes of the Romantics of the preceding generation, Delacroix and Préault to say nothing of Ingres and his imitators, these three submissions to the 1847 Salon displayed a desire for an almost aggressive naturalism.

## Realisms

Others during the Second Empire, such as Fromentin, Regnault or Ribot, were to follow on the same track without rejecting all idealisation, unlike Courbet. There are more links between the Romanticism of 1830 and the art of the 1850s than one imagines. As with all major aesthetic changes, Realism achieved some of the possibilities which had been latent in Romanticism: its concern for the distinctive nature of objects and persons, its search for a new spontaneity in the creative act and the goal of finding an archaic mythological repertoire in the real world, whether in nature or in country folk. Fontainebleau Forest and the peasant rooted in the country was the answer for one of the strongest trends in French painting at a time in its history when anything was possible. Unlike Antigna (*Lightning*, L'Éclair, Salon of 1848),

**Camille Corot**
*The Dance of the Nymphs*
(La Danse des nymphes)
1860-1865
oil on canvas

**Narcisse Diaz de la Peña**
*Fontainebleau Forest*
(Forêt de Fontainebleau)
1868, oil on canvas

Tassaert (*An Unhappy Family*, Une Famille malheureuse, Salon of 1949), Pils (*The Death of a Sister of Charity*, La Mort d'une sœur de charité, Salon of 1850-51) or the first Jules Breton, painters of urban poverty and domestic tragedy, with few exceptions, Millet and Courbet abandoned the city. This choice, linked to the regionalism of the time and the rediscovery of folklore, is an indication of their deep attachment to rural values, a disquiet in face of the impact of the industrial revolution and a supposed return to primal forces. The people and folk traditions, which Courbet drew upon to free himself from academism, seem to have been a refuge for painting which sought to recapture an authenticity. It was not just a question therefore of being 'more true', beyond what Romanticism had allowed itself in reaction to Neo-Classicism, but of communicating the sense of an integral purity through the representation of the countryside at work and landscapes spared from the urban scourge. In this respect, the great surge of momentum in landscape painting starting in the 1830s and names such as Corot, Théodore Rousseau or Diaz, cannot be separated from the Realism which emerged twenty years later. Furthermore, Millet and Courbet needed no more than to paint the Normandy fields or the area around Barbizon or Ornans, surrounded by limestone cliffs, to express the essentials. Occasionally political, often social, Realism moved beyond the circumstances which gave it rise.

Stéphane Guégan

**Octave Tassaert**
*An Unhappy Family*
(Une famille malheureuse)
1849
oil on canvas

**Charles-François Daubigny**
*The Harvest*
(La Moisson)
1851, oil on canvas

**Alexandre Antigna**
*Lightning*
(L'Éclair)
1848
oil on canvas

# DELACROIX AND ORIENTALISM

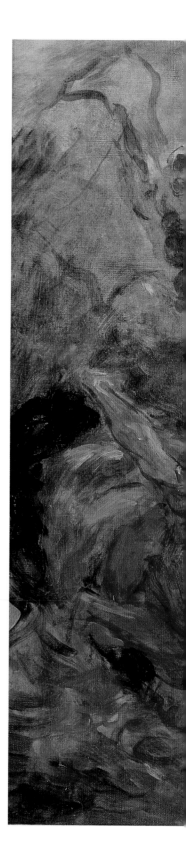

Orientalism, inseparable from colonial conquests and the simple thirst of the Western imagination, has been constantly reinvented throughout French art. The contribution of the Romantics to this call of the exotic is well represented in the collections: both Delacroix and Chassériau spent several weeks in the Maghreb. Delacroix was dazzled by his discovery of Morocco in 1832, Chassériau by his trip to Algeria in 1846. Each in his own way was seeking "the living, striking sublime with which the streets here are full and which kills you with its reality". From this experience, they drew subject matter, new climates, figures from another age through which to interpret ethnic differences and establish a rapport with the world of North Africa. The intensity of these paintings is not limited to capturing the Mediterranean light in all its splendour: as much as it affirms a specific reality, this work seeks to astonish, to make one dream. Others who followed, from Regnault to Guillaumet, not to mention Renoir at the start of the 1880s, strove to 'remake' the East. To rid it of clichés, as stated by Fromentin, the apologist of the aristocratic and nomadic life of the multi-faceted Algeria where he spent so much time.

S. G.

**Henri Regnault**
*Execution without Judgment under the Moorish Kings of Granada* (Exécution sans jugement sous les rois Maures de Grenade)
1870, oil on canvas

*The Lion Hunt* (Chasse aux lions) *is
a veritable explosion of colour [...].
Never have more beautiful, more intense
colours penetrated right to the soul through
the medium of the eyes.*

(Baudelaire, 1855)

**Eugène Delacroix**
*The Lion Hunt*
(Chasse aux lions)
1854
oil on canvas

# PHOTOGRAPHY FROM 1839 TO 1870

**Thibault**
*The Barricades on the*
*Faubourg du Temple after*
*the Attack, Monday,*
*26 June 1848*
(Barricades du faubourg
du Temple après l'attaque,
lundi 26 juin 1848)
1848, daguerreotype

From the invention of photography in 1839, photographers set off to explore the world. The daguerreotype produced isolated images, for example of the 1848 Paris barricades, the first image of an historical event to be reproduced in the press. With photography on paper, photo reports followed one after another: in 1851, the 'Heliographic Mission' documented the historic monuments of France due for restoration; and Maxime du Camp's coverage of Egypt and the Middle East – the first of its kind. For all of these official commissions, photographers were given the means and showed themselves all the more inventive as they explored virgin territory in the arts. This didn't stop them from frequently borrowing from painting or printing, as with Félix Nadar and Cameron in their development of the portraiture of artists and great men. In the reverse sense, the simplification of form and the flattening of perspective achieved by the lens clearly, if unconsciously, encouraged a generation of Impressionist painters to adopt a style of representation more faithful to the eye than to the imagination. By 1870, many technical advances had been made, including the perfecting of heliogravure, the first step towards the publication of works. Photographers henceforth held biennial Salons. At the same time, starting in 1855, studios were transformed into commercial enterprises which were to further gain in importance from 1870 onward.

Françoise Heilbrun

**Gustave Le Gray**
*Fontainebleau, a study
from nature*
(Fontainebleau,
étude d'après nature)
ca. 1850, proof on paper
from a waxed paper
negative

# GUSTAVE **COURBET** (1819-1877)

The Orsay collections provide thorough proof of Courbet's desire to make his mark on all styles of painting. His stunning submission to the 1850-1851 Salon, his 'exposition of principles', was the *Burial at Ornans* (Un enterrement à Ornans). A great moment in modern history, without heroes or pomposity, it was first entitled 'a painting of human figures, the account of a burial at Ornans'. Traditional idealisation and heroics were no longer necessary for large-scale painting. An anonymous funeral party in black clothes and white bonnets became a subject of universal import. This painting was realist, a term used at the time which Courbet disliked, in its rejection of the conventions rather than through any deliberate illusionism. In each of his paintings, from immodest nudes to bracing landscapes, from hunting scenes to rolling waves, Courbet sought to construct his vision of the nineteenth century with a straightforwardness tinged with lyricism. Here, the subject, sometimes considered banal, is as important as the language of the forms which always include strong contrasts, are powerfully executed and arranged in almost sculptural groups. It is easy to see why the next generation, Manet as well as Monet, would follow his lead without imitating him.

S. G.

**Gustave Courbet**
*The Cliffs of Étretat
after the Storm*
(La Falaise d'Étretat
après l'orage)
1870, oil on canvas

Mr Courbet has taken his place
in the current French School like
a canon ball that's just lodged
itself in a wall.

(François Sabatier, 1851)

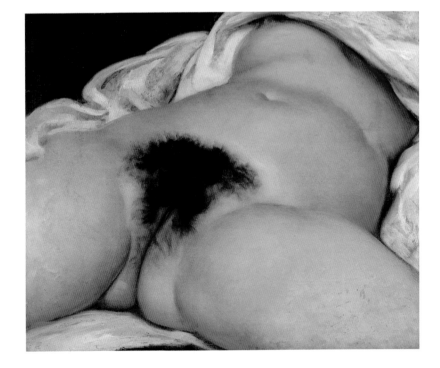

**Gustave Courbet**
*A Burial at Ornans*
(Un enterrement à Ornans)
1849-1850
oil on canvas

**Gustave Courbet**
*The Origin of the World*
(L'Origine du monde)
1866
oil on canvas

# JEAN-FRANÇOIS MILLET (1814-1875)

**Jean-François Millet**
*A Winnower*
(Un vanneur)
1866-1868, oil on wood

The son of well-to-do farmers from Gruchy, Millet (1814-1875) received a good education. Throughout his life, he read Virgil in the original, quoted Montaigne, and drew upon the Bible. Nearby Cherbourg provided a major step in his career as a painter. The city museum, particularly its Spanish collection, and his first drawing lessons encouraged his move to Paris as early as 1837. Twenty years later, he exhibited *The Gleaners* (Les Glaneuses). In the intervening years, his work underwent a complete change. He had begun with small canvasses of licentious pastoral subject matter in the style of the most colourful Romantics such as Boucher and Fragonard. But shortly before 1848, his peasants lost their pastoral air. *A Winnower* (Un vanneur), with its Michelangelo-like power in the archaic gesture, was a key point in this development. At the outbreak of cholera a year later, Millet fled to Barbizon, close to landscape artists such as Rousseau, where he began his 'period of the fields', more solemn and sorrowful than joyous. This world of labour, between biblical fatalism and simplicity, was to be echoed in the Naturalism of the end of the century (Bastien-Lepage, Lhermitte, Roll...) as well as in the work of Van Gogh.

S. G.

**Jean-François Millet**
*Spring*
(Le Printemps)
1870-1873, oil on canvas

*I do not want to end this list [...]
without hailing the arrival of
a great painter who, in wooden
shoes, follows in the footsteps
of Michelangelo and Lesueur.*

(Edmond About, 1857)

**Jean-François Millet**
*The Gleaners*
(Les Glaneuses)
1857
oil on canvas

# FROM PRÉAULT TO CARPEAUX

As with Delacroix in the field of painting, Rude, the author of *Napoleon Awaking to Immortality* (Napoléon s'éveillant à l'immortalité), and Préault represent the Romantic movement at Orsay. Since it was a question of working in inert marble or bronze, sculpture held out longer against the new styles of expressive reality, movement and violent sentiments. Daumier, with his *Ratapoil* and *The Celebrities of the Juste-Milieu* (Célébrités du juste milieu) opened the new route of Realism. The works of Carpeaux, who contributed to the greatness of the Second Empire, can be seen in the central walkway of the museum in the form of models, all the more precious since the 'definitive' versions have deteriorated, as can be seen in *Imperial France Bearing Light to the World and Protecting Agriculture and Industry* (La France impériale portant la lumière dans le monde et protégeant l'Agriculture et l'Industrie) in the Flore Pavilion. On the other hand, it's the original stone of *The Dance* (La Danse), commissioned by Garnier for the Paris Opera, which henceforth benefits from the air-conditioning and natural lighting from the vault.

Anne Pingeot

**Auguste Préault**
*Ophelia*
(L'Ophélie)
1842-1876
bronze

**Honoré Daumier**
*André Marie Jean Jacques Dupin,* also known as *Dupin the Elder*
(André Marie Jean Jacques Dupin, *dit* Dupin aîné)
1831-1835, coloured unfired clay

*The Opera façade is almost outraged by the wild passion with which Carpeaux' sculpture sways its hips.*

(Gautier, 1872)

**Jean-Baptiste Carpeaux**
*The Dance*
(La Danse)
1863–1868
stone

# 3

# Classic
# Modernism

**Pierre**
**Puvis de Chavannes**
*Young Girls by*
*the Seaside*
(Jeunes Filles au bord
de la mer)
1879, oil on canvas

**Alexandre Cabanel**
*The Birth of Venus*
(La Naissance de Vénus)
1863
oil on canvas

# 3 | Classic Modernism

Too often judged in terms of the banal works
which filled the walls of official exhibitions,
the Second Empire actually gave birth to numerous
masterpieces which mixed originality with a respect
for the Classical tradition.

In 1848, Jean Auguste Dominique Ingres, already sixty-eight years old, ex-student of Jacques Louis David, hero of the Salons of the Empire and former prestigious director of the French Academy at Rome, was a benchmark in the Parisian art world. Very early on, he distanced himself from Davidian formulae and, to the great displeasure of the the academic institutions, developed his classical heritage. He was happy to air his unorthodox views as in 1848, for example, when in common accord with Delacroix he supported the abolition of the Salon jury. However, when in 1863 Napoleon III wanted to impose the reform of arts education, Ingres took up his pen in defence of the academic tradition.

## Ingres and the 'grand genre' tradition of historical painting

If the portrait sculpture he was familiar with from his training at the Paris École des Beaux-Arts and the Italian paintings he had carefully studied maintained a presence in his work in the form of quotations and references, Ingres revitalised them through innovative plastic alternatives. His simplification of forms and of the backgrounds in which he set his models, the serpentine harmony of his line and the chromatic refinements which earned him the nickname of 'a Chinese lost in Athens', are clearly visible in *The Source* (La Source), begun in 1820 and modified several times before its completion in 1856.

**Théodore Chassériau**
*The Tepidarium*
(Tepidarium)
1853
oil on canvas

*I've never had
a success like this
one and without,
thank God, getting
more conceited.*

(Ingres, 1856)

**Jean Auguste
Dominique Ingres**
*The Source*
(La Source)
1820-1856
oil on canvas

Just as important to the understanding of the developments in Ingres' career is the unfinished painting exhibited under the title of *Venus at Paphos* (Vénus à Paphos). Begun by Ingres around 1852/53, the landscape was painted by his student Blaise Alexandre Desgoffe. Initially commissioned as a portrait, the original concept, particularly the anatomical distortion of the chest, was rejected, thus prompting this iconographical makeover full of innuendo. Desgoffe (represented at Orsay primarily through his still lifes of precious objects grouped in elaborate compositions imbued with a seventeenth-century Flemish and Dutch influence) was one of the many students and imitators, referred to as 'Ingrists', who surrounded Ingres in Paris and Rome and preserved the academic tradition at least throughout the Second Empire, applying it strictly or attempting to instil it with new life.

One of Ingres' oldest students – who moved in an eclectic circle since he has also been linked with Delacroix and Gustave Courbet – was Paul Chenavard, of Lyons, whose philosophical exaltation found an outlet in enormous canvasses for the moral edification of the viewer. His *Divina Tragedia*, part of an ambitious decorative project for the Pantheon, purports to be an allegorical illustration of the end of the religions of antiquity and the advent of the Christian Trinity. His academic training is clear in the many references which can be spotted at the heart of

**Jean-Achille Bénouville**
*View of a Roman Villa*
(Vue d'une villa romaine)
1844
oil on canvas

**Jules-Élie Delaunay**
*The Plague in Rome*
(La Peste à Rome)
1869, oil on canvas

this burgeoning mass of often strange figures handled with a great economy of colour in a crystalline atmosphere.

Faced with this grandiose vision heightened by new plastic accents, the *École des Beaux-Arts* trained a number of new recruits to perpetuate a certain iconographical tradition, as evident in the 1851 work by François Léon Bénouville, *Martyrs Led to their Execution* (Martyrs conduits au supplice). His younger brother sought above all to maintain the tradition of classical landscape, reworked in the studio, in paintings such as his 1844 *View of a Roman Villa* (Vue d'une villa romaine) which perfectly reflects academic injunctions regarding the positioning of forms and colours.

## Between Historical Subjects and Genre Scenes

Théodore Chassériau, another precocious student of Ingres, assured a continuity of tradition while at the same time giving art a new lease of life. He retained a somewhat abstract ideal from his master but rekindled it with the passion of Romantic concepts. This can be seen in his 1855 literary evocation of *Macbeth and the Three Witches* (Macbeth et les sorcières), in the flamboyant orientalism of *Arab Tribal Chiefs Challenging Each Other in Single Combat* (Chefs de tribus arabes se défiant en combat singulier) exhibited at the 1852 Salon, and even more so in his *Tepidarium* (Tépidarium), shown at the 1853 Salon, the result of a long period of matura-

# 3 | Classic Modernism

**Hippolyte Flandrin**
*Prince Napoléon*
1860
oil on canvas

**Jules-Élie Delaunay**
*Charles Hayem*
1865
oil on canvas

**Pierre-Jules Cavelier**
*Cornelia, Mother
of the Gracchi*
(Cornélie,
mère des Gracques)
1861, marble

tion following his discovery of the ruins of Pompeii in 1840. Beyond its sculptural references to antiquity (the standing, stretching figure of *Vénus de Milo*, facing the viewer), this scene of a rejuvenated and thus modern antiquity, is "a pretext for the exhibition of women of all sorts" in which the critics saw behind each chaste unveiling "provocative airs which conjure up visions of Capua". Such innovative painting played a part in supplanting the traditional hierarchy of genres which left the viewer hesitating between historical and genre painting.

Sculpture long maintained the survival of Neo-Classicism in works such as Pierre Jules Cavelier's 1861 *Cornelia, Mother of the Gracchi* (Cornélie, mère des Gracques). It featured Neo-Grec archaeology alongside a sometimes more austere Neo-Roman aspect (*The Reaper*, Le Faucheur, 1855, Eugène Guillaume). An early intrusion of Naturalism in a work of historical tendency, the 1865 evocation of the archaeological digs of Pompeii by Édouard Sain is matched by the sculpture of *A Find at Pompeii* (Une Trouvaille à Pompéi) by Hippolyte Moulin,

also thoroughly marked by the academic tradition. However, slightly later than in painting, the traditional teaching of the École des Beaux-Arts was to be submerged by the Romantic wave as seen, for example, in Auguste Préault's *Ophelia* (Ophélie) which he worked on from 1842 to 1876.

At a time when ceremonial portraiture had an important social function, Ingres, the celebrated portraitist, was assured a long legacy. Exhibitions were overrun with portraits of female subjects dressed in all their finery and of men in more austere clothing (*Prince Napoléon*, by Hippolyte Flandrin, 1860). Artists strove to outdo each other in the precision of the settings of their subjects and their rendering of anecdotal detail (*Charles Hayem*, by Jules-Élie Delaunay, 1865), sometimes at the expense of psychological acuteness (*Madame Barbe de Rimsky-Korsakov*, by Franz-Xaver Winterhalter, 1864). Similar conclusions can be drawn about portrait sculpture in which pale imitation is sometimes seen alongside brilliant invention such as in Carpeaux's 1862 bust of *Princess Mathilde*.

**Franz-Xaver Winterhalter**
*Madame Barbe de
Rimsky-Korsakov*
1864, oil on canvas

**Jean-Léon Gérôme**
*Jérusalem*
1867
oil on canvas

## Mythologies

Olympian goddesses were highly popular at the time and several versions of Venus – who needed only a large stretch of water to appear before the eyes of a captivated public – could be found in every exhibition. Alexandre Cabanel's *Venus* of 1863, lying on the waves surrounded by cherubs, appealed through the smoothness of its modelling and the sensitivity of its tender colours. His *Paolo et Francesca* of 1870, in a more contrasting range and a more lively composition, appears to pay homage to a painting of the same name by Ingres, but its imposing scale and theatrical grandiloquence distance it from the successes of the master.

Two celebrated artists of the 1860s, armed with a solid academic training, were to develop their art off the beaten track. The first, Gustave Moreau, through the use of an abundant iconographical repertoire drawn from his vast learning, developed a mythological symbolism (*Jason*, 1865, or *Orpheus*, Orphée, 1865) which was to have no followers. The same applied to Pierre Puvis de Chavannes whose work in fresco and as a decorative artist (panels for the decor of the Hôtel Vignon, 1866) is reflected in the economy of his palette and the rigour of his compositions.

From the fall of the monarchy to the fall of the Empire in 1870, arts institutions remained unchanged, advocating a uniform classical style. But this was in no way a constraint as much as a set of rules to which some conformed and which others sublimated. The view of this period is too often reductive. Upon study, one has to admit that tradition and modernity managed to go hand-in-hand.

Dominique Lobstein

*What's sure is that his exceptional, curious and polished talent interests, surprises, makes one dream and provokes a feeling unlike that of so many other irreproachable canvasses.*

(Gautier, 1866)

**Gustave Moreau**
*Orpheus*
(Orphée)
1865, oil on wood

# INGRES AND HIS IMITATORS

In 1999, the Ingres Museum in the painter's hometown of Montauban devoted an exhibition to the students of Ingres, those numerous young artists whom he taught his passion for line at the Paris Ecole des Beaux-Arts, from 1825 to 1834, and, from 1834 to 1841, at the Villa Medici, where the highly prized places were won through the Prix de Rome. Sometimes nicknamed 'the little soldiers of monsieur Ingres', more often known collectively as 'Ingristes', they assured the long survival of the principles and methods of the Master. Many remained remarkably faithful, resisting the temptations of Realism and Romanticism in order to maintain the cult of Ideal Beauty as developed in the studio. Amaury-Duval was among these. Both in his *Annunciation* (L'Annonciation) of 1860 and his portrait of *Madame de Loynes*, dated 1862, one finds the same insistence on the graphic aspect of the subject and the spatial gradation of the composition as propounded by the Master.

D. L.

**Eugène-Emmanuel**
**Amaury-Duval**
*The Annunciation*
(L'Annonciation)
1860
oil on canvas

**Eugène-Emmanuel**
**Amaury-Duval**
*Madame de Loynes*
1862
oil on canvas

**Jean Auguste**
**Dominique Ingres**
*Venus of Paphos*
(Vénus à Paphos)
1852-1853
oil on canvas

# FRENCH SCULPTURE (1848-1870)

The nineteenth century venerated the past to the point of creating a style called *Historicism*. The Classical tradition was renewed following Pradier, whose *Sappho* (Sapho) was the last masterpiece. Eugène Guillaume, who went furthest in the direction of antiquity, was the most awarded during his lifetime. Gabriel-Jules Thomas brought Ingres back to life with his *Virgil* (Virgile). But little by little, the influence of the Italian Renaissance developed. Paul Dubois, not having won the Prix de Rome, went to Florence to copy fifteenth-century frescos. The slender freshness of his *Florentine Singer* (Chanteur florentin), the result of his wide culture, won him the gold medal at the 1865 Salon. He follows the group from Toulouse : Alexandre Falguière, whose *Winner of the Cockfight* (Vainqueur au combat de coqs) recalls Jean de Boulogne's *Mercury* (Mercure); Antonin Mercié, whose *David* paid homage to Donatello. Michelangelo then seized the imagination. Eugène Delaplanche's *Eve After the Sin* (Ève après le péché) bends over in remorse, while Charles – René de Paul de Saint-Marceaux' *Genius Guarding the Secret of the Tomb* (Génie gardant le secret de la tombe) whirls about.

A. P.

**Gabriel-Jules Thomas**
*Virgil*
*(Virgile)*
1861, marble

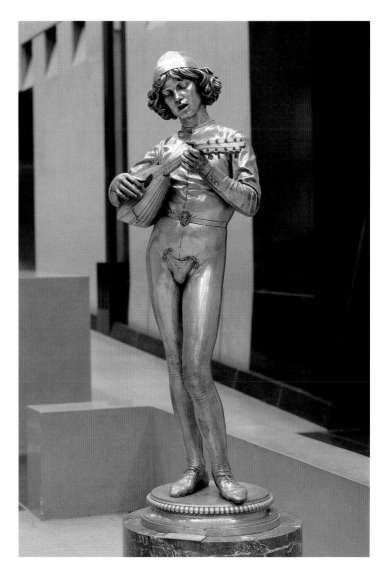

**Paul Dubois**
*Fifteenth-century*
*Florentine Singer*
(Chanteur florentin
du xvᵉ siècle)
1865, silvered cast

**Alexandre Falguière**
*Winner of the Cockfight*
(Vainqueur
au combat de coqs)
1864
bronze

# PIERRE **PUVIS DE CHAVANNES** (1824-1898)

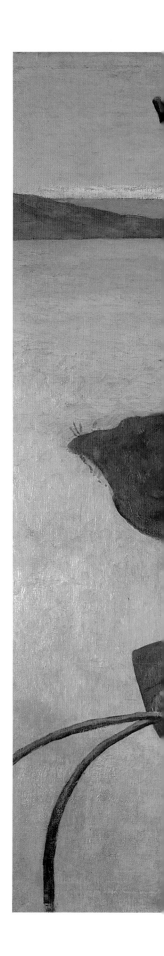

**Pierre
Puvis de Chavannes**
*The Young Mother* also
known *as Charity*
(La Jeune Mère
*dit aussi* La Charité)
ca. 1887
oil on canvas

**Pierre
Puvis de Chavannes**
*The Poor Fisherman*
(Le Pauvre Pêcheur)
1881, oil on canvas

The variety and quality of his work account for this artist's place among the top ranks in art history. Simplification of form and colour, an absence of depth, the importance placed on drawing and the use of solid blocks of colour typify his art.  His work is often allegorical, and the Franco-Prussian war inspired several of his paintings including *Hope* (L'Espérance), the embodiment of France following the 1870 war. Here, the frontal silhouette of the figure stands out clearly against the background. *Young Girls at the Seaside* (Jeunes Filles au bord de la mer) is one of his masterpieces: these three impassive figures in a stylised landscape open themselves to all interpretation; the pale colours, without any modelling, link harmoniously together. No anecdote, no realism, a monumental presence is expressed through its broad technique and fresco-like matte rendering. *The Poor Fisherman* (Le Pauvre Pêcheur) is particularly well-known, with its enigmatic subject, scholarly composition and unrealistic colours in a space brought back to the vertical. This painting heralded Symbolism: taken up by Seurat in his Hommage à Puvis de Chavannes, copied by Maillol, it stunned Gauguin, Hodler and the nordic painters as well as Picasso who owed to it the inspiration for his 'blue period'.

Serge Lemoine

49

# 4 The New Painting: The Time of Manet

**Édouard Manet**
*The Picnic* (detail)
(Le Déjeuner sur l'herbe)
1863
oil on canvas

**Édouard Manet**
*The Fifer*
(Le Fifre)
1866
oil on canvas

# 4 | The New Painting: The Time of Manet

Stuck between the tradition of Ingres, the Romantic legacy
of Delacroix and the Classical training of the École des
Beaux-Arts, young painters of the 1860s became aware
of an impending threat of ossification. Manet stands out
as the leader of a new school which reinvented Realism.

To escape the prevailing conformity, some turned to the museums to study the old masters directly and find their own way forward. Degas and Manet distinguished themselves as key figures of this new generation. Through the example of the Venetians and Rubens to which Gustave Moreau, his mentor in his Italian period, introduced him, Degas was able to rid himself of "this insipid, trivial drawing, à la Flandrin or Lamothe, and this dull grey colour", as taught by his professors (letter from Auguste de Gas to his son, November 1859). To see nature in masses rather than in detail, to reread the human form through an understanding of Michelangelo, Rubens and Correggio, these were the first steps in an apprenticeship which would lead him to the more radical lessons of the Quattrocento and antiquity.

Freed by these crucial discoveries, Degas was able to reinvent historical painting by composing ancient scenes midway between dreams and theatre design. His *Semiramis Building Babylon* (Sémiramis construisant Babylone) attests to the combined influence of Carpaccio's colourful cities, Moreau's vision of the Middle-Ages and decor designed by Puvis de Chavannes. Degas tackled all subject matter, refusing to pigeonhole himself in accepted traditional categories, as exemplified in *Family Portrait* (Portrait de famille) whose monumental scale was normally reserved for historical painting. In this bourgeois scene, with its theatrical quality, individualism asserted itself as the corollary of modernity. The expressive force of this painting won for Degas the title of modern primitive.

## The Salon

Still attached to his former masters but radically revolutionary in his painting method, Manet established himself at the forefront of a new school which attracted artists disgusted by the mawkishness of the Salon – the highly sought-after venue where Manet wished to exhibit his paintings. Oft rejected, his works triggered violent debate at the Salon des réfusés in 1863 where he showed his *Bathers* (Le

**James Tissot**
*Portrait of Mademoiselle
L.L.* also known as
*Young Woman in Red
Jacket*
(Portrait de M^elle L. L.
*dit aussi* Jeune Fille
en veste rouge)
1864, oil on canvas

*The two sisters* [The Bellelli Family] *by Mr E. Degas – a beginner who displays remarkable aptitudes – indicate an accurate feeling for nature and life on the part of the painter.*

(Castagnary, 1867)

**Edgar Degas**
*The Bellelli Family*
(La Famille Bellelli)
1867
oil on canvas

**Henri Fantin-Latour**
*Studio in the Batignolles*
(Un atelier aux
Batignolles)
1870
oil on canvas

Bain), better known today as *The Picnic* (Déjeuner sur l'herbe). This painting was as shocking for its subject matter as for its size, its sketchy execution, approximate perspective and artificial light. In the eyes of his contemporaries, this scene, based on Marcantonio Raimondi's engraving of Raphael's famous *Judgement of Paris*, was provocative from several points of view. How could a naked woman staring at the spectator in a titillating way, in monumental scale, and in the presence of two clothed men, be justified? Deaf to the artist's explanations of a modern Giorgione, the critics rejected this transposition of Renaissance idealism.

Manet repeated his challenge to tradition a few months later in his painting of an even more scandalous nude. His references to Goya's *Maja desnuda*, to Titian's *Venus*, Ingres' courtesans or Delacroix's colourful exoticism

were not enough to tone down the provocative nature of *Olympia*, "a monster of mundane love".

Was this the new painting? – a prostitute offered up to the gaze of all in the rawness of electric light? Amidst the tumult of protest set off by this painting, the voice of Zola rose in defence of the artist. Focussing on parts of the canvas rather than its subject matter, he wrote: "patches of light, luminous colours were called for, and you painted a bouquet; black patches were needed, and in one corner you placed a black woman and cat." The novelist points here to an important element of this new painting. His analysis voiced the opinion of a group of painters close to Manet celebrated in Fantin-Latour's famous *Studio in the Batignolles* (Un atelier aux Batignolles) painted just before the group was broken up by the Franco-Prussian war: Manet, shown at his

easel, is surrounded by Zacharie Astruc, Otto Schölderer, Renoir, Zola, Edmond Maître, Bazille and Monet.

## Scenes of contemporary life

Anxious to escape the bourgeois realism which was taking over portraiture and genre painting, innovative artists found a myriad of ways to rejuvenate this age-old art form. Manet favoured a dark background, grey or black, in order to reinforce the flatness of his figures, which he represented almost like playing cards. He also used the artifice of decor to highlight the individuality of his subject, as in his portrait of Zola. This was the method most commonly adopted by the new generation, as was the attention given to the sitter's costume which, if nothing new, was part of the charm of the upper-class Empire bourgeoisie as depicted by Carolus-Duran or Tissot. In his account of the 1864 Salon, the critic Léon Legrange said of Tissot's *Young Woman in Red Jacket* (Jeune fille en veste rouge), that it was "a model of elegance, of nobility, of simplicity." The

interest in the female toilette inspired several of Monet's masterpieces, including *Women in the Garden* (Femmes au jardin) in which patches of light colour stand out against a dense background of foliage. Four life-sized crinoline dresses, worn by undifferentiated models, seem to have a life of their own. As Zola wrote, "One must particularly love ones times to dare such a tour de force, to show fabric cut in two by shadow and sunlight, well-dressed ladies in a flower bed which the gardener has carefully raked."

**Édouard Manet**
*Émile Zola*
1868
oil on canvas

**Édouard Manet**
*Olympia*
1863
oil on canvas

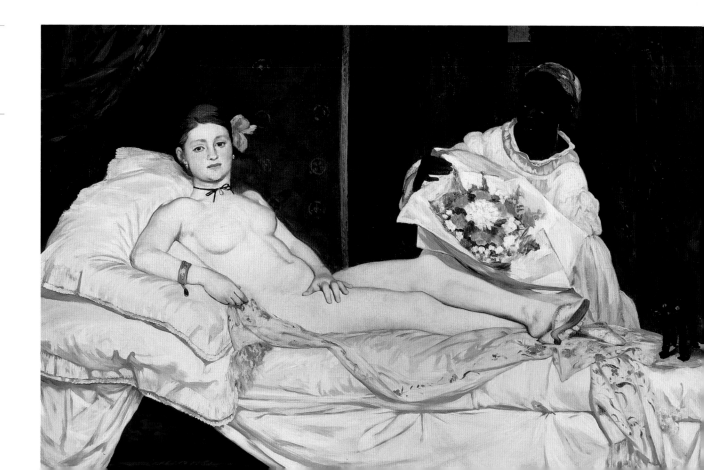

**Claude Monet**
*The Magpie*
(La Pie)
1868-1869
oil on canvas

**Eugène Boudin**
*The Beach at Trouville*
(La Plage de Trouville)
1864
oil on canvas

The desire to keep as close as possible to natural vision is equally clear in the slices of life painted by Degas who didn't hesitate to crop his figures in an incongruous way to give them the flavour of a scene caught on the spot. This method gives a surprising autonomy to the legs of the dancers moving about above the musicians in *The Orchestra of the Paris Opera* (L'Orchestre de l'Opéra). The influence of Japanese prints – with their abolition of the third dimension, the representation of space through the overlaying of picture planes, the simplification of colours – and of photography is behind these daring cut-outs.

## The Open Air

Divided between artifice and nature, painters of the 1860s also renewed landscape painting through their interest in the open air. Nature became the subject matter in and of itself, no longer as with the Romantics because of the emotions it evoked. The Norman beaches and sky painted with exceptional constancy by Boudin aroused the enthusiasm of Baudelaire at the 1859 Salon: "These studies, so rapidly and faithfully sketched, of what is the most changeable and most elusive in form and colour, of waves and clouds, always bear in the margin the date, the time, the wind condition [...]."

Through his influence, Monet in his turn became interested in the intangible elements of nature of which he sought to give living impressions. During the winter of 1869 in Honfleur, he painted a large snowscape entitled *The Magpie* (La Pie). In an immaculate setting void of any spatial reference point, the black and white bird, the only living thing in this glacial wasteland, has alighted on a fence. In the wintry light, the snow is coloured in a multitude of nuances. This painting, in its modernity and charm, is considered a milestone of Impressionism and is also one of the masterpieces of the Orsay collections.

Isabelle Cahn

**Claude Monet**
*Women in the Garden*
(Femmes au jardin)
1867
oil on canvas

# ÉDOUARD MANET (1832-1883)

Having tried the life of a sailor, Manet (1832-1883), the son of upper-class Parisians, served a six-year artist's apprenticeship in the studio of Thomas Couture. Through his travels in Holland, Germany, Italy and, later, Madrid, he discovered the art of the Old Masters which, along with the vogue at the time for Spain, left their mark on his first works. Though Baudelaire did not see him as 'the painter of modern life', he was enthusiastic about his painting of a dancer, *Lola de Valence*.

Often rejected by the Salon because of his deliberate improprieties, Manet was admired by a new generation of artists for his formal simplification and his elegant brushwork. His art of understatement gives his figures a strangeness and a timeless charm, clearly visible in the people in his *Balcony* (Le Balcon). Though he continued painting scenes of Parisian life, after 1870, through his contact with Monet, Manet tended towards open air painting. He adopted a light colourful palette, his brushwork became fragmented, and his Japonism more radical. Close to the Impressionists, he nevertheless refused to exhibit with them, concentrating on the Salon to make his name. At the time of his death, his work continued to stir controversy but was admired by the greatest artists of the time.

Isabelle Cahn

**Édouard Manet**
*Lola de Valence*
1862
oil on canvas

**Édouard Manet**
*At the Beach*
(Sur la plage)
1873
oil on canvas

**Édouard Manet**
*The Balcony*
(Le Balcon)
1868-1869
oil on canvas

# JAMES MAC NEIL WHISTLER (1834-1903)

**Henri Fantin-Latour**
*Homage to Delacroix*
(Hommage à Delacroix)
1864
oil on canvas

There is hardly a more cosmopolitan painter than James MacNeil Whistler (1834-1903). Born in Massachusetts but educated in Saint Petersburg and Paris, a student like Renoir of the Neo-Grec Charles Gleyre, Whistler rapidly moved in the circle of Bohemian Realism where, in the shadow of Courbet, other young men, notably Fantin-Latour and Legros, formed a new group. To this was added his first visits to London whose banks of the Thames and mysterious fogs were to long haunt his work. In the early 1860s, Whistler was also to discover Pre-Raphaelite painting there. The work of Millais and of Rossetti contributed to his move away from an art that he came to see as too objective. His universe of languid women or distilled landscapes is the result of a poetry of halftones, with a musical resonance reflected in the titles of his paintings. In 1863, his *White Girl* (Fille blanche, Washington) shared with Manet's *Déjeuner sur l'herbe* the honour of a scandal at the Salon des Refusés. The following year, Fantin-Latour brought these two stars of the new painting together in his *Hommage à Delacroix*. But unlike the painting of Manet, Whistler's was to continue refining itself down, in the spirit of all-pervasive Japonism. With his careful framing, daring cropping, heightened space and cloudy abstraction, Whistler, who signed himself with a butterfly, took wing.

S. G.

**James Mac Neil Whistler**
*Variations in Violet and Green*
(Variations en violet et vert)
1871, oil on canvas

**James Mac Neil Whistler**
*Arrangement in grey and black nº1* or *The Artist's Mother*
(Arrangement en gris et noir nº1, *ou* La Mère de l'artiste)
1871, oil on canvas

# THE FRIENDSHIP OF RENOIR, BAZILLE, MONET

**Claude Monet**
*The Picnic* (central part)
(Le Déjeuner sur l'herbe)
(partie centrale)
1865-1866
oil on canvas

**Pierre-Auguste Renoir**
*Frédéric Bazille*
*at his Easel*
(Frédéric Bazille
peignant à son chevalet)
1867
oil on canvas

During the summer of 1865, three young students of the Gleyre studio, Renoir, Bazille and Monet, met in Chailly-en-Bière, a village on the edge of the forest of Fontainebleau, to paint en plein air – in the open air. Impressed by Manet's *The Picnic* (Le Déjeuner sur l'herbe), Monet undertook a monumental canvas (4.60 x 6 m) on the same subject in which he included the figures of Courbet, seated next to his new companion Camille Doncieux, and his friend Bazille. The work was suddenly interrupted by an injury: laid up in bed at an inn, it was the turn of Monet to become Bazille's model for his *Improvised Field-Hospital* (Ambulance improvisée). The close collaboration between the three artists reveals itself as well in Renoir's portrait of Bazille painting a heron, a subject he himself had included in one of his still lifes during this period. Each of them however maintained his own personality. Bazille's landscapes and his portraits set in the open air have a photographic realism which distinguishes them from Monet's suggestive style or Renoir's sensuality. Bazille did not take part in the rich pictorial dialogue which brought Monet and Renoir together at the baths of La Grenouillère in Chatou in 1869. His tragic death during the Franco-Prussian War put an end to the intense relationship of this trio.

I. C.

*Until now I've enjoyed myself painting
the interior of my studio with my friends.
Manet is painting me.*

(Bazille, 1870)

**Frédéric Bazille**
*The Bazille's Studio*
(L'Atelier de Bazille)
1870
oil on canvas

# JAPONISM: THE ROUSSEAU SERVICE

*This admirable and unique service, decorated
by Bracquemond with Japanese motifs
borrowed from the farmyard and fish ponds,
the most beautiful recent tableware
I've had the pleasure to see.*

(Mallarmé, 1871)

Little by little by dint of its purchases, the Musée d'Orsay has reconstituted the Rousseau service which numbers more than forty pieces, round and oval platters, plates and assorted cups and jugs, down to a knife-rest and butter dish in keeping with the art of the table during this golden age of French cuisine. At the 1867 World Fair, this set drew the attention of critics of the avant-garde. It owed its success to its freshness and, at a time when the taste for the new Orient was at its height, to its Japonism. "People were going round all the shops in search of the latest arrivals, boxes with their fine engraving, sculpted playthings, lacquers decorated with stunning drawings [...] which flew off the shelves at crazy prices," wrote Astruc. Félix Bracquemond, the great enthusiast of Japanese art who designed the service for Eugène Rousseau, was also a friend of Manet: they can both be seen in Fantin-Latour's 1864 *Hommage à Delacroix*. From the Japanese prints which were to so interest the Impressionists and then Van Gogh and Gauguin, he drew a vocabulary of animals and principles of synthetic script. On the white background of dishes and platters, on the sides of lightly tinted enamelled glasses, he gave free rein to his imagination with a simplicity which became a reference point. Space and form were revolutionised. The Empire of the Rising Sun had conquered old Europe.

S. G.

**Félix-Henri
Bracquemond,
François-Eugène
Rousseau**
*Oval plate decorated with
a swallow and a waterlily*
Pattern designed in 1886,
China with underglaze
printed decoration

**Félix-Henri
Bracquemond,
François-Eugène
Rousseau**
*Round plate*
Pattern designed in
1866-1875, China with
underglaze printed
decoration

**François-Eugène
Rousseau, Appert
frères**
*Vase* ('teardrop' model)
ca. 1875-1878
tinted, engraved, painted,
enamelled and gilded
glass

# THE ARTS AND CRAFTS MOVEMENT

The Arts and Crafts movement played a fundamental role in the history of modern functionalism. Starting in 1848, it took root in Great Britain through the studies of Augustus Welby Pugin and the theoretical writings of John Ruskin, the great champion of Pre-Raphaelite painting (John Millais, William Hunt, Dante Gabriel Rossetti, etc.). In both cases, the pursuit of a more natural art based itself on an idealised vision of the Middle Ages. With the values of what one supposed a more united and healthy society, the medieval model led to the elaboration of a furniture of pure lines whose principles of construction were exposed and condition the final appearance, and of objects to embellish and edify the everyday world. A company established in 1861 by William Morris, friend of the Pre-Raphaelites and particularly Burne-Jones, sought to combine

craftsmanship, formal minimalism, organic references and even ecology and socialism. "The perception and creation of beauty are as necessary to man as his daily bread." But the company's production was most often too expensive and original to reach the working classes, ill prepared to support this new aesthetic. The Arts and Crafts movement was however to inspire other utopias right through to twentieth-century Bauhaus. Once past a short period of disfavour, it has since enjoyed unfailing success in England.

S. G.

**William Morris**
*Two hangings, 'Bird'*
*pattern designed*
*in 1877-1878*
wool

**Auguste Welby Pugin**
*Table*
1846-1850
pine, brass

*By a painting,
I mean a beautiful
romantic dream
of something which
has never and will
never exist.*
(Burne-Jones)

**Edward
Coley Burne-Jones**
*The Wheel of Fortune*
1875-1883
oil on canvas

# 5 The Impressionist Gallery

**Pierre-Auguste Renoir**
*The Swing*
(La Balançoire)
1876
oil on canvas

**Claude Monet**
*Saint-Lazare Station*
(La Gare Saint-Lazare)
1877
oil on canvas

Thanks to the generosity of numerous collectors beginning with
the Caillebotte bequest, the Musée d'Orsay today holds the most
beautiful collection of Impressionist paintings in the world.
The modernity of the artwork shines in all its glory under
the natural light of Orsay.

This is one of the most popular parts of a visit to Orsay – and for good reason: in the light of day, the Impressionist Gallery resembles some of the most significant paintings or sculptures of the art movement it houses. Two masterpieces mark its beginning and its end: Fantin-Latour's *Homage to Delacroix* (Hommage à Delacroix) in 1864, and, thirty years later, Cézanne's *Woman with a Coffee Pot* (La Femme à la cafetière). Between the two lies the history of Impressionism, heir of the great Romantic colourist, returning in the end to the Classical route through the Master of Aix.

Enduring in terms of its influence, the movement itself was actually short-lived if one limits oneself to the eight collective exhibitions held at irregular intervals between 1874 and 1886. But, when speaking of Renoir and Monet, Degas and Caillebotte, Pissarro and Cézanne, can one really speak about a coherent uniform movement, of a group of individuals bound by a common aesthetic faith? Nothing could be less certain. The rehanging in progress, that is, the regrouping of canvasses in a succession of monographical rooms which began with Monet and Renoir, demonstrates more than ever the diversity of languages and of universes at the heart of what we agree to call Impressionism, in the singular.

### The New Wave

The name which was at first pejorative has become today a guarantee of public success. Let's consider how this reversal come about. On 15 April 1874, in the old studio of the photographer Nadar, at 35 Boulevard des Capucines, an association of artists opened an exhibition, without state aid nor the approval of the French Institute. One woman, Berthe Morisot, and about thirty men had formed a co-operative "at their risk and peril", as Burty wrote the next day. There was no jury, no prizes: even the hanging of the works was drawn by straws. "The rooms, hung in reddish brown wool, highly favour the painting," Burty added. "The group which has thus offered itself up for debate is pursuing, with clearly recogni-

**Berthe Morisot**
*The Cradle*
(Le Berceau)
1874
oil on canvas

*The idea, the first idea was to remove
the wall which separates the studio
from daily life.*

(Edmond Duranty, 1876)

**Claude Monet**
*Luncheon in the Garden*
(Le Déjeuner)
1873
oil on canvas

**Camille Pissarro**
*Hoarfrost*
(Gelée blanche)
1873
oil on canvas

sable personal aims, a common artistic goal: in execution, the rendering of the wide open-air light; in feeling, the clarity of the immediate sensation." Many of these paintings which in 1874 "seemed to declare war on beauty" (J. Claretie) can be seen on the walls of Orsay – from Paul Cézanne's *The Hanged Man's House* (La Maison du pendu) to Pissarro's *Hoarfrost* (La Gelée blanche), from Monet's large *Luncheon in the Garden* (le Déjeuner) to Morisot's *Cradle* (Le Berceau). The lively hostility this exhibition provoked is an important element in the Impressionist legend. As caricatures attest, the canvasses were mocked as looking like confused rough sketches, monstrous embryos, slapdash paintings, unformed and unfinished. The press was though less malicious than is commonly supposed. The irony of someone like Louis Leroy about Monet and Pissarro is undeniable but is partly the result of the inherent insolent tone of a paper like Charivari in whose pages the movement was baptised. Leroy's celebrated charge against *Impression: Sunrise* (Impression, soleil levant, Claude Monet, Musée Marmottan, Paris) could equally have been applied to *Regatta at Argenteuil* (Régates à Argenteuil), also painted in 1872 in the same economical style: "Impression – I knew it. I said to myself, since I'm impressed, there must be an

impression in it. "Pissarro's *Hoarfrost* (La Gelée blanche) was greeted with even more hostility: "Those are furrows? That's frost? [...] These are just palette scrapings uniformly placed on a dirty canvas. There's no head, no tail, no top, no bottom, no front, no back... Perhaps, but the impression is there. Well, well, it's a funny thing, impressions." Besides Burty, mentioned above, other critics got out the kid gloves. This was Prouvaire writing about Morisot's *Cradle* (Le Berceau): "Nothing is at the same time more true and tender than this young mother [...] leaning over the cradle where her rosy child falls asleep." Until 1886 when the first paintings by Seurat and Signac became the object of the press' bad temper, Impressionism continued to meet with a mixed reception, which varied according to the artist; Degas,

**Paul Cézanne**
*The Hanged Man's House*
(La Maison du Pendu)
1873
oil on canvas

**Alfred Sisley**
*Snow in Louveciennes*
(La Neige à Louveciennes)
1878
oil on canvas

for example, had to endure less sarcasm from the press than Cézanne.

### Recognition

Very early on however, this light painting, so incorrect in the eyes of the critics, found its first collectors. Orsay's Impressionist Gallery owes much to them and preserves the memory of those, Moreau-Nélaton, Personnaz or Doctor Gachet, whose lucidity is all the more admirable given the total lack of interest in these new realists shown by the public authorities under Mac-Mahon and Grévy. In their time, Delacroix and Courbet had never met with such indifference. These art lovers, whose names are commemorated at the entrance of certain rooms and at the bottom of plaques, got around institutional resistance in the end. In 1890, as the result of a subscription lead by Monet which he had established twenty-five years earlier, Manet's *Olympia* crossed the threshold of the Luxembourg Museum, supposed in any event to provide an account of contemporary art from Louis XVIII onwards… Four years later, the Caillebotte donation, sixty-six canvasses strong but reduced to forty-one by the directors, was accepted with ill grace. This was the core around which was built the collection, unique of its kind, now housed in and enriched every year by the Musée Orsay. As early as 1876, Caillebotte, painter and friend of painters, decided to test the State by giving them his paintings so that "in the Luxembourg and later in the Louvre […] the public will – I won't say understand – but acknowledge this painting." His wish was to be fulfilled beyond all imagining. But success was long in coming, and some, like Sisley, didn't have as much time to enjoy it as Monet

**Alfred Sisley**
*The Flood at Port-Marly*
(L'Inondation à Port-Marly)
1876
oil on canvas

and Renoir. Today this painting stands out so clearly, it is hard to understand that it wasn't always the case.

Some claimed as their heritage the Barbizon landscape painters, Millet and Courbet; others positioned themselves in the footsteps of chroniclers of the city and modern lifestyles; the painters who formed the Impressionist group reoriented Realism, ridding it of all pomposity and lyrical effusions. It was appropriate for them not just to look at the world around them; it was important to look in a new way, with the freshness and almost the feigned naivety of Japanese etchings. Nothing is more mused upon than that spontaneous impression, the chance fleeting perception of the world, of the suburban countryside, or of Haussmann's Paris, in which one breathes freely. Through new ways of cropping an image and new perspective effects, by making the brushstroke and pure tones shimmer, they sought less to definitively capture a stable and orderly world than to embrace the constant metamorphosis of phenomena under the solar light or in the harsher brilliance of the recently invented electricity. To restore pattern to the movement of sight itself, to mix spontaneity and subjectivity in the rapid capturing of the subject, even if it meant reworking it in the studio, this was doubtless the prime objective of the landscape painters. Monet's *Water Lilies* (Les Nymphéas) series was to push to its furthest limits this pursuit of every-changing reality. The traditional distance between the artist and reality was being broken down. But it must not be forgotten that Impressionism did not limit itself to the championing of open-air painting or fragmented brushwork. Degas found his 'human comedy' far from the banks of the Seine, in the cafés or bordellos, at the opera, on the boulevards. A colourist and heir of Ingres, his painting is sharper, fiercer even. To some extent, Caillebotte was to follow his lead. Impressionism was clearly a big family.          Stéphane Guégan

**Edgar Degas**
*The Tub*
(Le Tub)
1886
pastel

**Claude Monet**
*Woman with Parasol*
(Femme à l'ombrelle)
1886
oil on canvas

# GUSTAVE **CAILLEBOTTE** (1848-1894)

Born to a family of very prosperous entrepreneurs, Gustave Caillebotte had no need to worry about the sales of his works during his lifetime. On the other hand, he was committed to helping his colleagues by buying their paintings and contributing to the organisation and promotion of Impressionnist exhibitions. He was long celebrated for his collection which he donated to the State in 1894 (among which were Manet's *Balcony* (Le Balcon); Monet's *Saint-Lazare Station* (La Gare Saint-Lazare); Renoir's *The Dance at the Moulin de la Galette* (Bal du Moulin de la Galette), and one painting, *The Floor-Scrapers* (les Raboteurs de parquets). Despite the provocative layout and naturalist subject matter, these sombre floor-strippers, rejected by the Salon and shown at the 1876 Impressionist Exhibition, had not yet completely distinguished themselves from the training of Bonnat, Caillebotte's teacher. A brilliant observer of urban life in transition who better than any other evoked modern Paris (*Rooftops under Snow*, Vue de toits, effet de neige), with his energy and tensions, his palette of clear matte tones, a painter of faces full of expressive tautness (the portrait of Henri Cordier), Caillebotte has become known to the public thanks to reproductions of his large compositions (*Paris: A Rainy Day*, Rue de Paris; temps de pluie, Art Institute of Chicago) and recent international retrospective exhibitions.

Anne Distel

**Caillebotte**
*Rooftops under Snow*
(Vue de toits, effet
de neige)
1878, oil on canvas

**Gustave Caillebotte**
*Henri Cordier (1849-1929)*
1883
oil on canvas

*Do nudes, gentlemen, if the nude
suits you [...]. But let your nude
be beautiful, otherwise don't bother.*
Louis Esnault

**Gustave Caillebotte**
*The Floor Scrapers*
(Raboteurs de parquet)
1875
oil on canvas

# Pierre-Auguste **RENOIR** (1841-1919)

Renoir is one of the most popular painters as well as one of the best represented in the Musée d'Orsay in terms of numbers (more than a hundred works in all techniques for one mustn't forget his works in sculpture) as well as in the variety of styles undertaken throughout the development of his long career, from one of his first Salon paintings, a portrait of his friend Sisley's father, William Sisley of 1864, to his ultimate masterpiece, *The Bathers* (Les Baigneuses), finished shortly before his death in 1919. Paintings such as *The Dance at the Moulin de la Galette* (Bal du Moulin de la Galette, 1876), *The Swing* (La Balançoire, 1876) or *Girls at the Piano* (Jeunes filles au piano, 1892) are without doubt among the most often reproduced works. Favouring the human face, Renoir's Impressionionism (he was one of the historic promoters of the 1874 exhibition) was from the start devoted essentially to the expression of colour, dissolving forms in a vivid shimmer. His phase, often referred to as 'Ingresque', of a self-imposed discipline of well-defined line – already detectable in 1883 in *Dance in the City* (La Danse à la ville) and *Dance in the Country* (La Danse à la campagne) but quite clear in the portrait of the young Julie Manet of 1887 – was only a pause for reflection leading to the jubilant effusions of the end of his life

A. D.

**Pierre-Auguste Renoir**
*Dance in the City*
(Danse à la ville)
1883
oil on canvas

**Pierre-Auguste Renoir**
*Torso*
(Torse)
ca. 1875-1876
oil on canvas

*The Moulin de la Galette is one of those complete summaries of fundamental observation and of a luminous atmosphere: the exhileration of the dance, of the noise, the sun, the dust of an open-air fête.*

(Gustave Geffroy, 1893)

**Pierre-Auguste Renoir**
*The Dance at the Moulin de la Galette, Montmartre*
(Bal au Moulin de la Galette, Montmartre)
1876, oil on canvas

# EDGAR **DEGAS** (1834-1917)

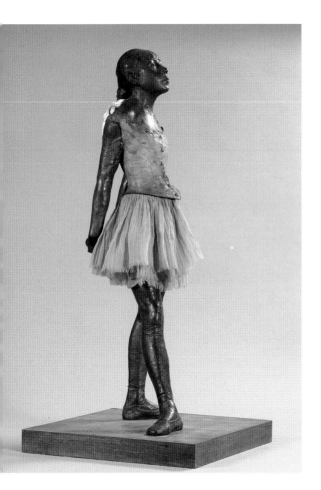

It is as easy to pick out the best, or at least the most significant or best-loved, paintings in the Musée d'Orsay by Manet, Monet or Renoir, as it is difficult to, if not impossible, with Degas. It's not for any lack of historically important works – Salon paintings (where he exhibited *The Bellelli Family*, (Portrait de famille – La Famille Bellelli in 1867) or those shown in Impressionist exhibitions (*The Absinthe Drinker*, L'Absinthe) – but the variety of techniques (various experiments in oil, pastel and sculpture), from very small-scale to monumental compositions, and the diversity of intentions (from the meticulous preciosity of *Dance Studio at the Opera on the Rue Le Peletier*, Le Foyer de la danse à l'Opéra de la Rue Le Peletier, to the provocative offhandedness of *The Absinthe Drinker*, (L'Absinthe) invite the viewer to follow along with the moods of Degas: the young artist who rivalled the old masters, the upholder of the 'new painting' who turns our received ideas about perspective upside down, the old man threatened by blindness who at the dawn of the twentieth century captured in a few pastel strokes the angular form of a dancer in leotard.

A. D.

**Edgar Degas**
*Little Dancer, Aged Fourteen or Large Dressed Dancer*
(Petite danseuse de 14 ans ou Grande danseuse habillée)
1932 (bronze edition)
bronze, lost-wax cast, patinated, tulle, satin

**Edgar Degas**
*Dance Studio at the Opera on the Rue Le Peletier*
(Le Foyer de la danse à l'Opéra de la rue Le Peletier)
1872, oil on canvas

**Edgar Degas**
*In a Café,* also known as *The Absinthe Drinker*
(Dans un café, *dit aussi* L'Absinthe)
ca. 1875-1876, oil on canvas

# CLAUDE **MONET** (1840-1926)

Claude Monet had a keen sense of history: disdained by the authorities and absent from the national public collections which otherwise included so many mediocre painters, he refused to rest until the one he considered his master, Manet, had received the respect due him. We are indebted to Monet for his impassioned and effective campaign of 1890 to acquire, through a group of subscribers (himself included), and donate to the State the master's Olympia. Monet was nearing his sixties when in February 1897 a selection of his canvasses chosen by the administration from amongst the works donated by his friend Gustave Caillebotte was finally exhibited at the Luxembourg Museum (the museum of contemporary art of the time). This could explain his reservations about the sale of his works to the State: one *Cathedral* (Cathédrale) in 1907, and *Women in the Garden* (Femmes au jardin), a painting from his early period which he had the satisfaction of selling at a very high price in 1921. We should however recall his munificent donation, through the persuasion of his friend Clemenceau, of his ultimate *Water Lilies* (Nymphéas) housed in the Orangerie in the Tuileries Gardens. Since his death, the Museum's collection of his works has continued to grow: amongst the most recent acquisitions by donation is the luminous *Poplars (wind effect)* (Effet de vent, série des peupliers, 1891).

A. D.

**Claude Monet**
*Poplars (Wind Effect)*
(Effet de vent,
série des peupliers)
1891, oil on canvas

**Claude Monet**
*Poppies*
(Coquelicots)
1881
oil on canvas

**Claude Monet**
*Blue Waterlilies*
(Nymphéas bleus)
ca. 1916-1919
oil on canvas

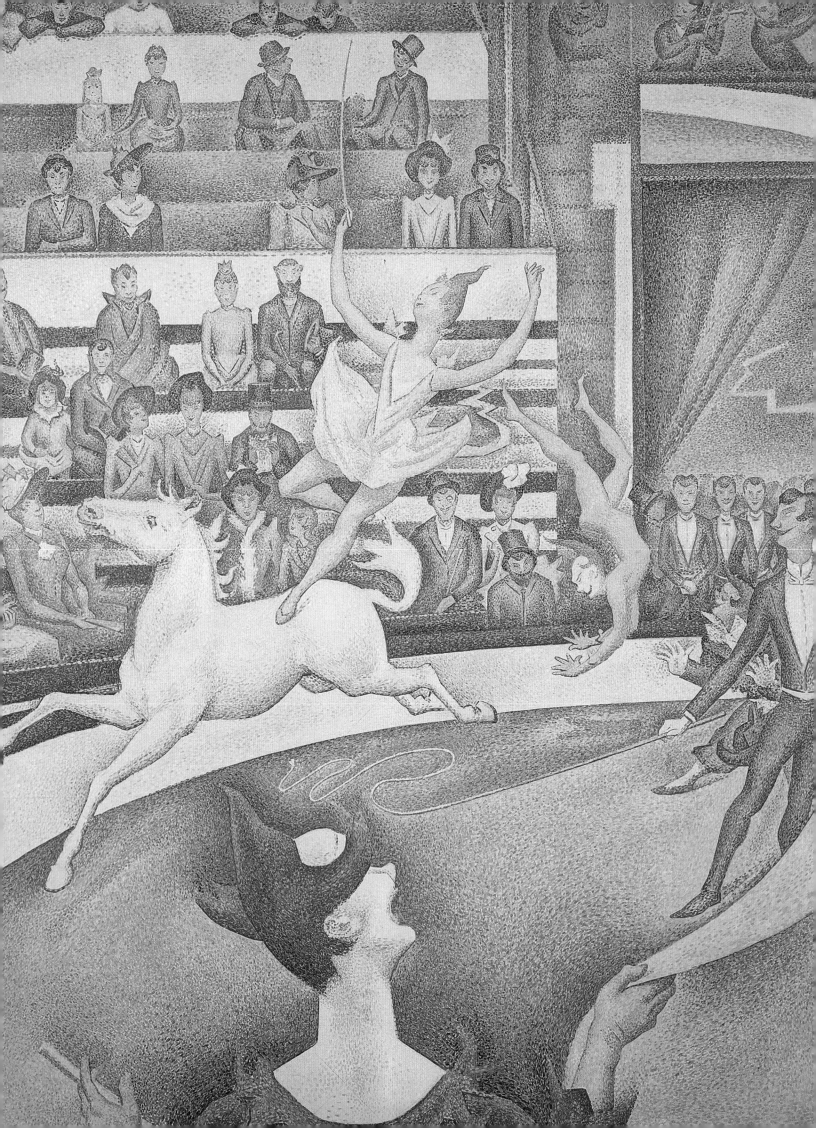

# 6 The Age of Iron, Art Nouveau

**Georges Seurat**
*Circus*
(Cirque)
1890-1891
oil on canvas

**Hector Guimard**
*Central panel from
a great balcony*
1905-1907, cast iron

# 6 | The Age of Iron, Art Nouveau

Already perceptible in the 1820s, notably in the vogue for the Neo-Gothic, the return of the decorative arts to historical styles reached its apogee after 1850.

The Neo-Classicism in fashion during the Empire did not hold out long against this resurgence of styles from a bygone France. This curious inversion of history was favoured by the availability from this point on of a design-book of all periods which was applied to furniture, goldsmithing and ceramics as much as to architecture. The nineteenth century had no style because it had all styles: this was the principal criticism made of the period from the reign of Louis-Philippe to the emergence of Art Nouveau fifty years later. This clearly paradoxical situation saw the Europe of the 1830s to the 1880s equipping itself with factories while at the same time furnishing itself in the style of Henri II or Louis XIII. But we mustn't take things at face value: historicism wasn't just a way to escape the modern world and retreat to 'the good old days'. The refusal to integrate the forms and structures of the nascent industrial civilisation into the decorative arts was not as straightforward as is generally supposed. For this eclecticism, a label which long burdened the composite taste of the period, was in no way a lazy repetition of outdated styles. On the contrary, it implied a free relationship with the old and the marriage between form and function.

Viollet-le-Duc's ideas, beginning in the 1830s and 40s, were to be enriched by the new historicism. As in England at the heart of the Arts and Crafts movement, the Middle Ages seemed the model of moral and functional probity. Structure and simplicity, according to Viollet-le-Duc, must take precedence over gratuitous ornament. To varying degrees, this balance is one of the forgotten elements of the eclecticism of the time. The influence of the Renaissance, Baroque, Rocaille or Louis XV, indeed of the Orient, did not prohibit invention. And the mechanisation of workshops contributed to the development of techniques and a growth in the luxury market. It was the period of the

**René Lalique**
*'Dragonfly' neck pendant*
1903-1905
gold, translucid enamel, brilliant, aquamarine

**Charles-Guillaume Diehl,**
**Emmanuel Frémiet**
*Medal cabinet*
1867
cedar, marquetry, walnut, ebony, ivory, bronze, copper, oak

**François-Désiré Froment-Meurice**
*Toilet Chest of the Duchess of Parma*
(La toilette de la Duchesse de Parme)
1845 (completed in 1851),
garnets, emeralds, glass, silver, niello, engraved iron, bronze, gilding, silvering, copper, enamel, grisaille, translucid enamel

arts applied to industry, of useful art, of chemical processes in silvering and gilding. But the career of the great Froment-Meurice shows that, without debasing itself, the arts could meet the new demand while satisfying the old elite with magnificent precious objects.

## A New Art of Living

The development of modern comforts in the home (heating, sanitation, etc.) was to be just as decisive a matter for reflection for the creators of Art Nouveau. The organic unity of space and its decoration was well in place before the blossoming of Art Nouveau, varying chronologically and aesthetically according to the European centre. In Paris, Nancy, Barcelona, Glasgow, Vienna or Prague, the light lines of Art Nouveau triumphed for two decades over the heaviness of official taste and the caution of an historicism which had had its day. The first Art Nouveau Salon organised in Paris by Samuel

Bing in 1895, was conceived as a voyage through varied techniques and materials. Furniture, stained-glass, tapestries and ceramics, signed by Van de Velde, Cros, Gallé, Tiffany, Lalique, Dalpayrat or Delaherche, illustrated the new aesthetic. Its characteristic supple lines inspired by vegetal curves, veins and stems were imitated in wood and metal, while the taste for asymmetry was borrowed from the Orient. Contrary to this amalgam of elements which illustrate the open nature of Art Nouveau as championed by Bing, Guimard undertook creations based on a greater stylistic unity. This 'architect of art', as he called himself, designed his buildings down to the

**Louis Majorelle**
*'Orchids' Desk*
ca. 1905-1909,
mahogany, rosewood,
gilded bronze, leather

**François-Rupert Carabin**
*Bookcase*
1890
walnut, wrought iron,
glass

smallest detail, including the interior decoration, in order to create an overall aesthetic programme. The ideal of a utilitarian art propounded by Victor Horta in Brussels inspired his Castel Béranger (1894-1896), on the Rue La Fontaine in Paris. He was not only responsible for the construction of the building but for the interior layout of its thirty-six flats. In 1898, he received the Grand Prix of the city of Paris for his façade of supple, asymmetrical lines in refined materials which stood out against the monotony of the street. Following this success, Guimard obtained the commission for metro entrances whose cast-iron vegetal undulations can still be seen today at certain stations.

### An International Outburst
While the capital was enthusing over 'femmes-fleurs', snail-like spirals, vines, orchids and lotuses transformed into jewel-lery, lamps or vases, in Nancy, Gallé presided over an Art Nouveau School whose influence was to become international. Bringing together industries and craftsmen, he created and distributed furniture of supple lines, and ceramics and polychrome

**Joseph Hoffmann**
*Chair with reclinable back, mahogany varnish*
design ca. 1908,
perforated plywood with mahogany finish, brass

glassware in abstract or symbolic decoration inspired by his long botanical meditations. Furniture of inlaid mahogany by Majorelle, water-lily lamps by Daum, pâte-de-verre decorative pieces by Dammouse and Décorchemont, favrile-glass by Tiffany – the creations of the Nancy School combined lightness, translucence and massiveness of materials. The dominant vegetal motifs of their shapes and ornaments were sometimes combined with elements from the Far East, Egypt or folk arts. But the imagination of Carabin went beyond accepted decorative limits when he included sculpted nudes in suggestive poses in his furniture constructed of disparate materials.

This emancipation of the arts gave rise to the birth of the Secession in Austria and central Europe, a reaction against the Biedermeier Style and the nationalistic retrenchment of the arts. 'To each century its art, to art its liberty' proclaimed the motto inscribed in gold lettering at the entrance to the pavilion of the Vienna Secession in 1898. Its members set up a review and exhibitions where all modern

Europe met to offer the Viennese public 'a clear vision of the evolution of artistic life'. In 1900 for example, the English Ashbee, the Belgian Van de Velde and the Scots Mackintosh showed together there, displaying a tendency towards geometric forms contrary to the more sinuous and suggestive taste of Gallé and Horta. This first associa-

tion was to lead to a second, larger collective undertaking with greater repercussions: the Wiener Werkstätte. Following the example of the Arts and Crafts movement and their refusal of mediocre mass production, Josef Hoffmann and Koloman Moser were to propose objects adapted to the needs of modern life with refined lines and in materials appropriate to mass production. Functional simplicity was all-determining. Abandoning for good the idea of a fusion with the forces of nature dear to the Franco-Belgian group, Hoffmann and Moser adopted an unembellished fluidity inspired by Japan which was to spread as far as the United States, as attested by the works of Frank Lloyd Wright and the entire Chicago School.

## Symbolism and Neo-Impressionism

During the period from 1880 to 1914, the situation of painting and sculpture was no less burgeoning and complex than the renewal of the decorative arts. 'Pompier' painting, the pejorative term for academic art, or more specifically Salon art, perpetuated an attachment to historical, mythological and allegorical subject matter and to the more or less ideal nude, without ever reinventing itself. Whether in the curse of Cain illustrated in great epic style by Cormon, in the meticulous illustrations of Paris life by Béraud close to the trompe-l'œil of coloured photographs, or in the sombre sober portraits by Bonnat, there was basically nothing very traditional about this work. Often banal, rarely inventive, it combined an antique Greco-Roman repertoire with the already accepted codes of Romanticism, indeed of the Realism of Courbet. For one mustn't forget the strong presence in the Salon of the masters of Naturalism, from Bastien-Lepage to Lhermitte and Roll, where hardworking rural France, honest in the face of harsh conditions, was showed off to the

**Charles
Rennie Mackintoch**
*Writing Desk*
ca. 1904, white lacquered
wood, tinted glass, steal,
lead, silvered brass

# 6 | The Age of Iron, Art Nouveau

**Félix Vallotton**
*Misia at her Dressing Table*
(Misia, à la coiffeuse)
1898, oil on canvas

**Aristide Maillol**
*The Mediterranean*
(La Méditerranée)
ca. 1905
marble

Paris public. Orientalism did not escape the fashion and artists such as Guillaumet, Dinet, Dagnan-Bouveret or Muenier were able to alternate between scenes of rural France and the archaic exoticism of colonial Algeria.

Different factors explain the appearance at the end of the 1880s of a Symbolist aesthetic. A new generation of painters and sculptors were at the same time opposed to the Salon, until around 1900 when some were accepted there, and to the different forms which Naturalism had taken, from academic painting to Impressionism. The reac-

tion was Europe-wide and based, according to the country, on a few examples from the preceding generation. In this respect, Odilon Redon, Pierre Puvis de Chavannes and Gustave Moreau were no less heralded as masters than were Baudelaire, Mallarmé or Verlaine in the field of poetry. The values of Romanticism, the concern to maintain an aesthetic of dream and suggestion, or to oppose the purity of an idealism of combat to the vulgarity of the times justified the rejection of all expression conditioned by the imitation of nature. By returning on the contrary 'to the mysterious centre of thought,' as Gauguin put it, the artist could free himself from illusionism in order to create coloured equivalents to the emotions, to the mysteries of the soul and, yes, even to the secrets of the invisible world. Sérusier and the Nabis subscribed by their own admission to a filiation with Gauguin and Émile Bernard before preferring to them, in the case of Maurice Denis, the more classic Cézanne.

The draw of the esoteric, accompanied or not by a sincere return to religion, was finally rejected by other members of the group, such as Bonnard, Vuillard and Vallotton. Their research, combined with a keen interest in stage design, decor and Japanese prints, led to an autonomous artistic style.

## Symbolist Thought

Truly nebulous, Symbolism eludes all strict definition. It even adapted itself to the imperatives of a more reassuring, comprehensible art than the barbarous audacity of Gauguin or the disquieting visions of Redon. The flights of imagination, the subtleties of consciousness, halfway between dream and sleep, took on evanescent forms under the brush of Carrière, sweet and melancholic forms under that of Henri Martin.

These dreamlike apparitions and brushes with the unconscious are echoed in the play of blended forms by the Italian sculptor Medardo Rosso. While Rodin interpreted the realm of the passions through expressive distortions, Maillol's sculpture seems full of internalised tension.

Symbolism was far from being the only answer to the Naturalism of the end of the century, nor was it the only road to renewal. The painting of Seurat and Signac offered another no less fertile route when one considers the repercussions of pointillism on the technique of Matisse, Derain and Vlaminck. Fauvism, which exploded on the scene at the Autumn Salon of 1905, owed much to the chromatic virulence of Gauguin and Van Gogh, and to the example of non-Western arts. In some respects, it was also one of the results of the developments in Neo-Impressionism starting in 1886, the date when *Sunday Afternoon on the Island of La Grande Jatte* (Un dimanche après-midi à l'île de la Grande Jatte) was shown at the last Impressionist exhibition. Following the premature death of Seurat five years later,

**Odilon Redon**
*Parsifal*
1912, pastel

**Pierre Bonnard**
*Child Playing in the Sand*
(L'Enfant au pâté de sable)
1894-1895
oil on canvas

André Derain
*Charing Cross Bridge,
London*
(Pont de Charing Cross,
Londres)
ca. 1906
oil on canvas

Signac, Cros and many others including the elderly Pissarro experimented in every way with the use of pure tones, of contrast in the combination of complementary colours, in their search for a more luminous, more emotionally pure painting. The subject matter – working-class life, the Normandy beaches, arcadian Tropez – was of little import; anecdote and the picturesque were rejected in order to let the specific methods of painting speak for themselves: colours and virtual lines, the dynamics of the picture. It is not surprising that the new avant-gardes, far from breaking with the despised nineteenth century, long made capital out of it.

Stéphane Guégan and Isabelle Cahn

Henri Matisse
*Luxe, Calme et Volupté*
1904
oil on canvas

*Right:*
Paul Signac
*Red Buoy, Saint-Tropez*
(La Bouée rouge,
Saint-Tropez)
1895
oil on canvas

# PHOTOGRAPHY FROM 1890 TO 1914

**George Henry Seeley**
*Tribute*
ca. 1907
gelatin silver print

This was a period full of revolutionary technical advances most of which, for social and economic reasons, could not be put into practice until after the First World War. Such was the case with the halftone process which enabled the reproduction of images without the need for engraving on wood; of the breaking down of motion which was to lead to cinema; of colour photography since at the turn of the century only the Lumière brothers' autochrome had been commercialised. The process of shooting a picture was greatly simplified by, for example, the marketing of portable snapshot cameras, making the 'eighth art' accessible to a new and extensive public. The period witnessed a new approach to photography reflecting private life (Bonnard, Vuillard, Zola) as well as fantasy (Jeandel), initiated as early as 1860 to 1870 by Lewis Carroll. There was at the time, on the one hand, large photographic companies, on the other, millions of amateurs. Some of the latter with artistic ambitions formed clubs which, starting in Europe at the beginning of the 1890s with Emerson and Evans, gave birth to the Pictorialist movement. Encouraged by the work of the 'painter-engravers', the Pictorialists favoured the primacy of a personal vision in their documentary transcriptions. They showed in international exhibitions, selected by jury, and were published in sumptuous reviews. Their pictures (Stieglitz, White) were strongly influenced by the works of the Impressionists and Symbolists. On the periphery of Pictorialism, Atget documented old Paris and its environs and left his mark on some of the greatest photographers of the twentieth century. With the exception of Coburn, British by adoption, Pictorialism led nowhere in Europe after 1914. In the United States however Stieglitz, Steichen and Strand were to do their best work following the First World War.

F. H.

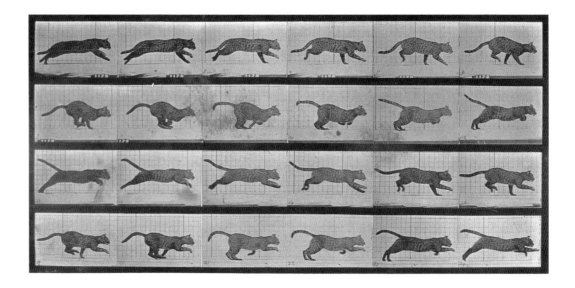

**Edward Muybridge**
*Cat Animal Locomotion*
ca. 1873
heliogravure 1887

**Alfred Stieglitz**
*Georgia O'Keeffe:*
*a Portait*
1918, gelatin silver print

# PAUL GAUGUIN (1848-1903)

Paul Gauguin (1848-1903) came to painting late in life. A former stockbroker and shrewd speculator, a life-long money man, he collected modern paintings and drawings, particularly Impressionist, before Pissarro taught him how to handle a paintbrush himself. It is not surprising that his first landscapes, beginning in 1873, should bear this influence, or that his interior scenes incorporate elements of Degas. The period from 1886 to 1888 marked a turning point with his discovery of Brittany, which he had imagined more archaic, and his meeting with Émile Bernard and Van Gogh. The first encouraged him to distill his painting down to a synthesis of the Japanese, the second drew him towards pure colour and Expressionism. This two-fold approach was to remain a constant with Gauguin. A self-avowed student of Puvis de Chavannes, he was only partly primitive. His barbarism, attributed to him as early as 1887 in Martinique, was not exclusive until his time in the Marquises. For if Gauguin was the first to openly draw upon non-Western arts, of Java and Tahiti, as attested in his brilliant *Oviri*, he did not reject the harmony of form and figure as much as has been claimed. Gauguin must be taken with all his contradictions, without which his Oceanic Eden would lose its spice.

S. G.

**Paul Gauguin**
*Oviri*
1894
stoneware, enamel

**Paul Gauguin**
*Self-Portrait as Yellow Christ*
(Autoportrait
au Christ jaune)
1889-1890
oil on canvas

**Paul Gauguin**
*The White Horse*
(Le Cheval blanc)
1898
oil on canvas

# Vincent **VAN GOGH** (1853-1890)

Van Gogh (1853-1890) was burdened by profound psychological illness; he did not owe his genius to his chronic dementia. Along with his friends Gauguin and Toulouse-Lautrec, he was one of the most cultivated artists of his generation, and one of the most lucid as well given the need to move beyond Impressionism. Having grown up in Holland in a family of pastors and art dealers, he hesitated a long time between the priesthood and painting before he turned the latter into a religion. An admirer of Millet as much as Rembrandt, his artistic education began in Brussels in 1880 under Anton Mauve, a landscape painter close to Barbizon. His first pictures, painted in the north, were dark, hard and harsh. In March 1866, he found himself in Paris working, like Toulouse-Lautrec and Émile Bernard, in the Cormon studio. Through Signac, he became interested in Neo-Impressionism and in Japanese crepon prints from which he drew trenchant colours, synthetic drawing and heightened space. He then found in the Midi the equivalent of the Orient of his dreams. In Arles, he worked with Gauguin, but arguments and illness put an end to their partnership in late 1888. He retreated to Auvers, near Doctor Gachet, where he freed himself from all attachments before bowing out.

S. G.

**Vincent Van Gogh**
*Starry Night*
(La Nuit étoilée)
1888
oil on canvas

**Vincent Van Gogh**
*The Bedroom*
(La Chambre)
1889
oil on canvas

**Vincent Van Gogh**
*Self-Portrait*
(Autoportrait)
1887
oil on canvas

# HENRI DE **TOULOUSE-LAUTREC** (1864-1901)

**Henri
de Toulouse-Lautrec**
*The Bed* (Le Lit)
1892
oil on cardboard

**Henri
de Toulouse-Lautrec**
*The Toilette* (La Toilette)
1896
oil on cardboard

Born to the old Albi aristocracy, Henri de Toulouse-Lautrec (1864-1901) moved in the circle of sleazy music hall habitués, people of the night and the circus, of boulevardiers and prostitutes. His early training with Princeteau, a good animal painter and horseman, as Toulouse-Lautrec was later to become, was followed in the mid-80s with work in the studios of, first, Bonnat, then Cormon. His future ease with body movement and the accentuation of faces and gestures is owed to these two official masters. His tendency towards strong outline and fierce light was reinforced by a critical discovery of Degas and Japanese etchings. A friendship with Van Gogh at one period clearly gave impetus to the development of his own very expressionistic style which was to have an impact on the young Picasso. Dancers and prostitutes, an alcoholic haze and electric colours, an economy of line and stridency of pure tones – the Spaniard was to borrow all of this on his arrival in Paris. Toulouse-Lautrec, exhausted by his unbridled lifestyle, died young; but not before he had worked in all genres, including posters and engraving, and had become one of the most important creators of the Moulin Rouge years and of the *Revue Blanche.*

S. G.

**Henri
de Toulouse-Lautrec**
*The Clown Cha-u-Kao*
(La Clownesse
Cha-u-Kao)
1895, oil on cardboard

# THE NABIS

The Nabis ('prophet' in Hebrew) were a group of former students of the Condorcet College and the Jullian Academy whose aesthetic was varied and adaptable. Bonnard, Vuillard, Maurice Denis, Vallotton and Maillol were its most well-known members. Others, such as Ker Xavier Roussel and the sculptor Georges Lacombe, were also linked to this decisive movement of 1890s modernity. They were allied in their common rejection of strict Naturalism which brought them, Sérusier and Verkade in particular, close to the School of Pont-Aven. The decorative vocation of painting was an article of faith which led them into the field of theatre, stage sets and posters, and of interior architecture. The Nabis, above all Denis and Vuillard, produced numerous, large-scale sacred and profane stage sets. Before it could illustrate any subject, painting had to speak through line and colour and its appropriateness for its setting. It was a question of revitalising the art of painting through a simplification of form and a free use of colour as learned from the work of the Italian Primitives, the Japanese and the example of a few modern artists, Puvis de Chavannes, Gauguin and Cézanne.

S. G.

**Paul Sérusier**
*The Talisman*
(Le Talisman)
1888
oil on canvas

**Maurice Denis**
*Climbing to Calvary*
(La Montée au calvaire)
1889
oil on canvas

*The more pure the elements,*
*the more pure the work.*

(Vuillard, 1890)

**Édouard Vuillard**
*In Bed*
(Au lit)
1891
oil on canvas

# Paul CÉZANNE (1839-1906)

The life of Paul Cézanne (1839-1906), the son of an Aix-en-Provence banker, spanned the period from the invention of photography to Cubism. This pivotal figure in the Impressionist adventure also wanted to "become classic again through nature, that is, through feeling." The influence of Delacroix and the great Venetians as well as Manet can be seen in his first paintings, violent in subject matter as well as in execution. He referred to this as his 'couillarde' (ballsy) period. A friend of Zola and Pissarro, in 1874 and 1877, along with the Impressionists, he exhibited canvasses as colourful but already more structured than theirs. After 1880 and his return to the Midi, his painting freed itself from the aesthetic of the fleeting moment and returned to the classic which he described: "Imagine Poussin completely reworked according to nature. That's the classic that I mean." Indeed, his religious views of the Sainte-Victoire mountain and his bathers at one with nature like fruit on a tree all bear witness to a more orderly, solar world. But beyond its insistent references and its distinctive modulation, Cézanne's style remains faithful to pattern and to the primacy of colour whose richness, as he said, endows a figure with all its fullness.

S. G.

**Paul Cézanne**
*Woman with Coffee Pot*
(La Femme à la cafetière)
1890-1895
oil on canvas

**Paul Cézanne**
*Bathers*
(Les Baigneurs)
1890-1892
oil on canvas

*It's like a playing card.*
*His red roofs against a blue sea.*
Cézanne

**Paul Cézanne**
*The Estaque*
(L'Estaque)
1878-1879
oil on canvas

# Auguste **RODIN** (1840-1917)

Rodin is at the same time the greatest artist of the nineteenth century and one of the greatest of the twentieth. Following the scandal of the *The Bronze Age* (L'Âge d'airain), his first statue accused of being modelled on nature, he created the teaming world of the *The Gates of Hell* (La Porte de l'Enfer) in which his admiration for Michelangelo led to the expressionism of the bodies. Destined for a museum of decorative arts once briefly envisaged for the site of the ruins of the Cour des Comptes, these gates on loan to the Musée d'Orsay from the Rodin Museum are now found in the place for which they were intended more than a century ago. Rodin was never to see it in bronze, nor his Balzac which the *Société des Gens de lettres* (the Society of Letters) had commissioned then rejected. This surging form, the symbol of creation, stands like a flame at the heart of the museum. Rodin's continued study of forms made him an artist of the twentieth-century: he honed down in order to express more. His *Man Walking* (L'Homme qui marche), composed of the legs of his 1880 *Saint John the Baptist* (Saint Jean-Baptiste) with the *Petit Palais Torso* (Torse), enlarged in 1905, was exhibited in Rome's Farnese Palace before coming to Orsay to demonstrate how this modeller of forms turned assembler made the transition from the previous century.

A. P.

**Auguste Rodin**
*The Bronze Age*
(L'Âge d'airain)
1877-1880
bronze

**Auguste Rodin**
*Honoré de Balzac*
1891-1898
plaster cast

**Auguste Rodin**
*The Gates of Hell*
(La Porte de l'Enfer)
1880-1917
plaster cast

**Ground floor**

# 0

**Pre-Impressionism**

Architecture
Decorative arts
Drawings, pastels
Paintings
Photographs
Sculptures

Artists
BARYE 2
BAZILLE 18
CABANEL 3
CARPEAUX Lille gallery
CHASSÉRIAU 2
COROT 5, 6
COURBET 7
DAUMIER 4
DEGAS 13
DELACROIX 2
FANTIN-LATOUR 15
GÉRÔME 1, 3
INGRES 1
MANET 14
MILLET 5, 6
MONET 18
MOREAU 12
MORRIS 27
MOSER 28
PUVIS DE CHAVANNES 11
VIOLLET-LE-DUC 25
WRIGHT 27 bis

Movements
ACADEMIC ART Lille
gallery, 1, 3
BARBIZON SCHOOL 5, 6

Collections
CHAUCHARD Seine gallery, 5
MOLLARD 20
PERSONNAZ 19
*Room being refitted*
15 to 17, 19 to 23

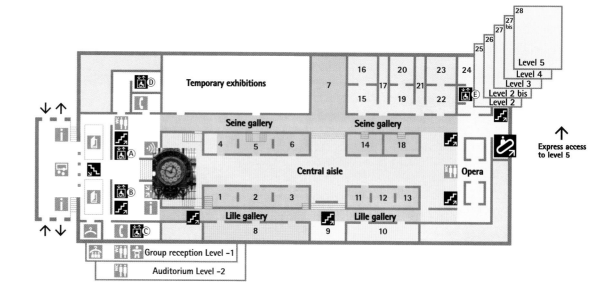

Express access
to level 5

Escalator — Stairs — Elevator

Information — Ticket window — Rest rooms — Changing table — Cloakroom — Group cloakroom

Telephone — Meeting point — Audioguide — Restaurant — Bookshop Cardshop Boutique — Viewpoint

# THE MUSÉE D'ORSAY - PRACTICAL INFORMATION

## Upper level
# 5

**Impressionism, Post–Impressionism**

Architecture
Decorative arts
Drawings, pastels
Paintings
Sculptures

Artists
CAILLEBOTTE 30
CÉZANNE 36, 41
DEGAS 30, 31, 33, 37, 38
DOUANIER ROUSSEAU 42
GAUGUIN 43, 44
MANET 29 à 31
MATISSE 46
MONET 29, 32, 34
PISSARRO 32
RENOIR 39
REDON 40
SEURAT 45
SIGNAC 45, 46
SISLEY 32
TOULOUSE–LAUTREC 36, 47
VAN GOGH 35
WHISTLER 30

Movements
PONT–AVEN 43, 44
NABIS 48

Collections
GACHET 41
KAGANOVITCH 50
MOREAU–NÉLATON 29

↓
Down to levels
4, 3 and 2

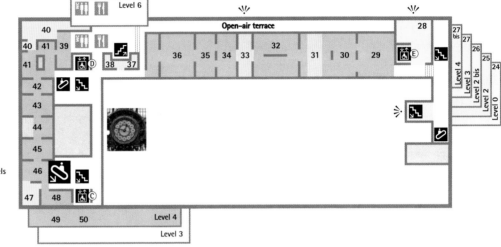

## Middle level
# 2

**Academic art, naturalism, symbolism, Art nouveau**

Architecture
Decorative arts
Paintings
Sculptures

Artists
AMIET 60
BÖCKLIN 59
BOLDINI 57
BONNARD 72
BOURDELLE Lille terrace
BURNE–JONES 59
CARRIÈRE 59
CLAUDEL Seine terrace
DALOU 56
DENIS 70
DETAILLE 55
GALLÉ 63
GAUDÍ 65
GUIMARD 61
HODLER 60
HOMER 59
KLIMT 60
KLINGER 59
MAILLOL Lille terrace
MUNCH 60
POMPON Lille terrace
RODIN Seine and Rodin terrace
VUILLARD 71

Movements
ACADEMIC ART 51
ART NOUVEAU 61 to 66
ECLECTICISM 52
JAPONISME 53
NABIS 70 to 72
NATURALISM 55, 56, 58
ORIENTALISM 54
SYMBOLISM 59, 60, 62

↓
Down to
the ground floor
and exit

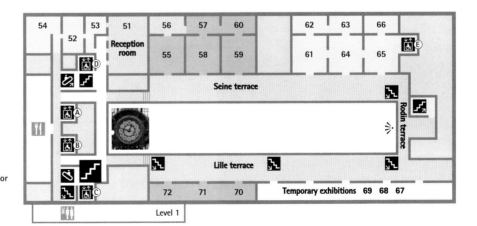

## Musée d'Orsay

62, rue de Lille
75343 Paris cedex 07

### Entrance

The main entrance
1, rue de
la Légion d'Honneur
75007 Paris

### Informations

Main telephone:
01 40 49 48 14
Individual Visitors'
Information Service:
01 40 49 48 00

Internet:
www.musee-orsay.fr

### Opening times

Monday: closed
Tuesday, Wednesday,
Friday and Saturday:
10am to 6pm; in summer,
open from 9am
Thursday: 10am to
9:45pm
Sunday: 9am to 6pm
Ticket sales close at
5:15pm (9pm on
Thursday)
Galleries start closing at
5:30pm (9:15 on
Thursday)

### Transportation

Buses: 24, 63, 68, 69, 73,
83, 84 and 94
Métro: line 12, Solférino
station
RER: line C, Musée
d'Orsay station
Taxis: Rue de Solférino
and Quai Anatole-France
Car parks: Deligny,
Louvre, Montalembert

### Entrance Fees

Full price: 7 Euros
Reduced rate and
Sundays: 5 Euros
Free admission: under
18s, 'Carte Blanche'
subscribers, members of
the Friends of the Musée
d'Orsay

### Restaurants and Cafés

• The Restaurant
Housed in the former
dining room of the Orsay
train station hotel, the
restaurant's exceptional
decor painted by Gabriel
Ferrier and Benjamin
Constant in 1900 is set off
by gilt-work, chandeliers
and mirrors.
Telephone:
01 45 49 42 33
Open Tuesday,
Wednesday, Friday,
Saturday and Sunday
from 11:30am to 2:30pm;
Thursday from 7pm to
9:15pm

• Tea Room: 3:30pm
to 5:30pm
(except Thursday)

### Restaurants and Cafés

• Le Café des Hauteurs
This relaxing area
shows the metal
structure of the building
to advantage and offers
a remarkable view over
the Seine through the
station clock.
The terrace, open
from May to October,
overlooks the magnificent
cityscape of the Right
Bank.
Open every day except
Monday from 10am
to 5pm, and on
Thursday to 9pm

• Quick Snacks on
the Mezzanine
Open every day (except
Monday) from 11am to
5pm; on Sundays and
in summer from 10am
to 5pm

## Bookshop - Postcard Shop - Boutique

The museum bookshop offers reference books on the period from 1848 to 1914 as well as CD-ROMs, videos, postcards, posters, reproductions, jewellery and gifts. Free access from 9:30am to 6:30pm, on Thursday to 9:30pm.
Information:
01 40 49 47 22

## The Auditorium

Paris' only wholly wooden concert hall, the Musée d'Orsay auditorium combines exceptional acoustics with the latest equipment. This 347-seat hall is the venue for a rich musical programme in connection with the permanent collections and temporary exhibitions. Film festivals, lectures and conferences are also held throughout the year.

## Services

• Audio guides available in six languages: French, English, German, Italian, Spanish, Japanese
• Cloakrooms
• Public telephones
• Post-boxes
• Pushchair loans
• Baby-changing tables

## Reduced Mobility Visitors

The museum is equipped with numerous lifts, automatic doors and access ramps. Wheelchairs are available in the cloakroom. A special plan of the museum for handicapped visitors is available at the information desks.

## Guided Tours

• Adult Visits
Either in groups or individually, guides enable visitors to discover the museum and its collections.

• Youth Visits
Discover an exhibition, learn how to look at a painting, find out how sculptors work... The museum welcomes children, on their own or with their family, to discover the fine arts of the second half of the nineteenth century.

• Sign-language visits are organised for adults and children.

## The Musée d'Orsay 'Carte Blanche'

This annual subscription card provides free access throughout the year, without queuing, to the museum collections and exhibitions. It includes many other advantages: free mailings, free or reduced rates for guided tours, concerts, etc.
Information:
01 40 49 47 28

## The Friends of the Musée d'Orsay

Through the acquisition of works of art and the promotion of patronage, the Friends of the Musée d'Orsay actively participate in the impact and development of the museum and contributes to the enrichment of its collections.
Lectures, visits in the company of exhibition curators, conferences and trips help establish a cultural link between members and the Musée d'Orsay.
Information:
01 40 49 48 34
www.amis-musees.fr
amiorsay@club-internet.fr

**Gustave Courbet**
*The Artist's Studio*
(L'Atelier du peintre)
1854-1855
oil on canvas

This issue is published under the management of Serge Lemoine, president of the Musée d'Orsay and Jean-Christophe Castelain, publisher of L'ŒIL

**Musée d'Orsay**
**Publications** Annie Dufour and Stéphane Guégan
**Communication** 01 40 49 49 20, presse@musee-orsay.fr

**L'ŒIL,** Art Revue founded in 1955.
Artclair Éditions - 21, rue Leriche - 75015 Paris. tel : 01 48 42 90 00
fax : 01 48 42 90 01 – e-mail : loeil@artclair.com.

**Publisher** Jean-Christophe Castelain.
**Editor in chief of L'ŒIL** Annie Perez, 01 48 42 90 19
Special issue : **Director** Stéphanie Pioda, 01 48 42 90 15.
**Partnership** Laure Desjonquères, 01 48 42 90 11.
**Contributing editors** Isabelle Cahn, Anne Distel, Stéphane Guégan, Françoise Heilbrun,
Serge Lemoine, Dominique Lobstein, Caroline Mathieu, Anne Pingeot.
**Sub-editor, iconographer** Pierre Morio, 01 48 42 90 13.
**Translation** Else - Janet Chevrier.
**Production manager** Pierre Ozanne, 01 48 42 90 17.
**Graphic design** Pascal Guédin. **Making up** Christine Marchandise.
**Photoengraving** Quatcoul. **Printed In Italy by** STIGE.

Joint commission 0208 K 82708. Copyright : April 2004. ISSN : 0029-862X.
ISBN L'ŒIL : 2-915479-06-2. ISBN Musée d'Orsay : 2-905724-04-8